INTRODUCTION

Italian food is some of the most delicious and varied in the world, so little wonder it's also one of the most popular. What's not to love about a place that invented pizza, lasagna, and tiramisu? *Chop, Sizzle, Wow* shows you how to re-create some of Italy's favorite dishes; it's a cool, comic-strip version of *The Silver Spoon*, a collection of recipes that was first published in Italy in 1950 and has pretty much been the bible of Italian cookery ever since. Like the Bible, it is very, very long, so we've picked out the best of the best. These fifty fast and simple recipes are all illustrated to show you, step by step, how to whip up an Italian feast at home.

HOW TO EAT THE ITALIAN WAY

To understand Italian food, you first need to understand Italians and what food means to them. They don't just love food; it is an art form, their "other" religion. You've only got to listen to a conversation in Italy—be it between people in the countryside or the city—to know that the main topic of discussion is what they'll be having for breakfast, lunch, or dinner, and where they'll be going to get it. In short, Italy is a nation obsessed with food, to the point of being fanatical.

Not so long ago, a well-known pasta manufacturer issued a list of "rules" to help teach foreigners how to avoid messing up when in Italy. It was all food-related of course, and it all came down to keeping things authentic. Why change something that is perfect in the first place? The first crime, unsurprisingly, is putting ketchup on pasta. This is viewed as one of the greatest "culinary sins," right up there with serving pasta like a vegetable or side dish. Pasta is something to be honored; the main event, if you will. It should come after *antipasti* (little appetizers) as *il primo* (the first course), and never *il secondo* (the second course, which would be meat, fish, or even just vegetables). After that, you might also have *insalata* (a salad course), *formaggi e frutta* (cheese and fresh seasonal fruit, always peeled), and *dolce* (dessert). Other sins include the combination of chicken and pasta—a major no-no, though it's unclear exactly why, the Italians just wouldn't do it—and a ban on adding oil to boiling water for pasta (it should be drizzled, in scant amounts, onto pasta after it's cooked to keep it moist and supple). Finally, what is probably the most important rule of all: Eating should never, ever be done alone. Italians believe the only way to show true respect for tradition, food, and the art that has gone into making it is by sharing it with those you love most.

You've probably guessed by now that mealtime in Italy is a sacred affair. Having plenty of time to savor it—two to three hours at least—is essential to fully appreciate every flavor and skill that has gone into putting the food on your plate. That Italians still place so much importance on breaking bread together is the key to their passion for the *dolce vita* (a sweet and happy life) and is also the underlying intent of *Chop, Sizzle, Wow*. The food you make will never taste as good as when you share it with family and friends.

LANDSCAPE AND CLIMATE

The huge variety of Italian dishes comes down to the country's immensely varied landscape and climate, and the fact that Italy wasn't a unified country until the early nineteenth century. Until then, each of the twenty regions we know today was effectively its own little country, brimming with unique flavors born out of having dramatically different landscapes. Italy is shaped like a long boot with a stiletto heel at the bottom. The top of the boot opens to the snowy, mountainous north, with its deep-green pastures and borders with France, Switzerland, Austria, and Slovenia. This region produces excellent dairy and meat products, while the hot, arid plains of the southern heel reach deep into the Mediterranean Sea towards Tunisia and are perfect for fruit orchards, tomatoes, and olive groves. In the center, the more temperate plains are the country's breadbasket, where wheat, corn, and barley flourish.

When you put all these products together, it's easy to see that real Italian cooking is still a largely artisanal affair. It is based on prime, seasonal, and local ingredients—never try to fob an Italian off with a tomato in February, or anything less than spring lamb (*agnello*) for Easter—and the majority of dishes are solid, hearty creations designed to nourish the body and nurture the soul. Have you ever noticed the general lack of Italian chefs and cooks fiddling around with foam and liquid nitrogen? That's because they

are far too busy sniffing out the best produce in local markets, or hanging out in the kitchen cooking and eating with their friends, or traveling the length and breadth of their country in search of the best Grilled Sardines (p. 58), Steak Pizzaiola (p. 52), or a perfectly made espresso—which, by the way, most Italians agree you'll find in Rome.

KEY INGREDIENTS

It comes as little surprise, then, to discover that each region has edible treasures that make it famous. Emilia-

Romagna, for example, is known for its strong, salty, raw cow's-milk cheese *Parmigiano-Reggiano* (Parmesan in English), Parma ham, and balsamic vinegar so rich and sweet you could almost drink it by the glass. Piedmont is famed for its fairy-tale oak, beech, and hazel forests that hide pungent, knobbly white truffles that are among the most expensive ingredients on earth (casino owner Stanley Ho reportedly paid $330,000 for two weighing a kilo each in 2010). Sicily, the biggest island in the Mediterranean, is the place to go for a pleasingly bitter, yet delightfully sweet, blood orange granita (like a grainy sorbet, see pp. 82–83 for how to make Strawberry or Apricot Granita) and decadent cannoli (sweet pastry shells filled with ricotta, see pp. 90–91). Tuscan olive oil is so sought-after that food criminals have been known to fake it. Products like these cause Italian hearts to break when they can't get them and chests to swell with pride when they can, and nearly all are protected by the DOP (*Denominazione di Origine Protetta*) stamp of quality. Look out for it when shopping for Italian ingredients. Otherwise, make like an Italian and swap the supermarket for farmers' markets and delicatessens. The quality is usually higher, it's often cheaper, and the staff will happily tell you which fruit and vegetables are in season and therefore what is tastiest. Better yet, most places will let you try a little nibble of something before you buy it, making shopping a whole lot more fun (and tasty!).

It won't be long before you learn what Italians have long known: When you can't be bothered to cook, just serve a plate of cheese (combine ricotta drizzled with truffle oil and mozzarella layered with tomatoes and basil, and add Gorgonzola for something strong and blue), *salumi* (preserved meats; try thin slices of salami, prosciutto, and bresaola), good bread and olives, and dinner is not only done, it's absolutely delicious. And nothing makes people happier than that.

REGIONAL DISHES

Sometimes it's time to get down to some serious cooking. *Chop, Sizzle, Wow* is split into chapters that cover appetizers (*antipasti*), pasta (*il primo*), main courses (*il secondo*), and desserts (*dolce*) to help you put together the ultimate Italian feast. The recipe selection focuses on the most celebrated dishes of different regions.

Florence is king for its one-pot, hunter's-style Chicken Cacciatore (p. 60). Naples is home to the classic Pizza Margherita (pp. 20–21), consisting of nothing more than a disc of flat, chewy dough topped with fresh tomato sauce and mozzarella, baked in a hot oven then strewn with fresh basil leaves. Legend has it that it was created in 1889 to honour the visiting Queen Margherita, who insisted that everything that passed her lips resemble the Italian flag! Tucked into the heel of Italy, Puglia is known for its stuffed Panzarotti (pp. 26–27), which look like a calzone and make excellent picnic food. The best Tagliatelle with Peas and Ham (p. 38) comes from Emilia-Romagna; while Carbonara (p. 41), only genuine when served with spaghetti, is a Roman dish. The classic Fritto Misto (pp. 66–67) is at its very best when using seafood hauled fresh from the lagoons of Venice. Twice-baked almond biscuits known as Cantucci (p. 74), called "coffee bread" in English because they are so good for dipping, are the medieval treasure of Prato, and creamy Panna Cotta with Hazelnut Sauce (pp. 78–79) is a treat from Piedmont, where the cooler climate makes for thick forests and lush green grass for better dairy cows. You could spend a lifetime cooking your way through the regional dishes of Italy and never get to the end, but *Chop, Sizzle, Wow* is a great way to start.

SHOPPING TIPS

When buying basic ingredients, keep it simple. You don't need to go in search of fresh pasta—most Italians prefer to use a good brand of dried pasta such as De Cecco—but do invest in good-quality olive oil and balsamic vinegar to keep at hand. Canned Italian tomatoes will almost certainly be better than any fresh ones you can buy out of season, but fresh herbs like basil, oregano, and sage will give your cooking a bright and lively finish that you cannot achieve with the dried versions. Ready-cooked canned beans these days are almost as good as dried and reconstituted, but fresh fish is always better than frozen, and a butcher will ensure you get the right cut of meat rather than you trying to find it in a supermarket refrigerator. If any recipe calls for wine, it can easily be replaced with stock or even plain old tap water.

COOKING AND TECHNIQUES

Luckily, because Italian food on the whole is so practical and down-to-earth, you won't need too much by way of special equipment. Sharp knives are essential, as are cutting boards, wooden spoons and a handheld balloon whisk. Find a heavy-bottomed pan for making risottos, a large

pan for boiling pasta in plenty of water or heating oil for frying, and a large shallow pan for cooking sauces. Invest in a solid baking sheet for roasting and (when it's turned upside down) for using as a pizza stone in a very hot oven. Add scales, a measuring pitcher, a cake pan, a set of ramekins, and a couple of mixing bowls

that can double as vessels for salads or desserts like tiramisu, and you're away.

The most important thing when cooking is to read the recipe thoroughly at the very start so you have an overview of everything you need to do. Then set your *mise en place*—that's chef talk for getting all the equipment together and your ingredients weighed and laid out ready for cooking. Heating the oven in advance, or having a bowl of ice water on hand to stop vegetables, cooking can make all the difference between success and failure. Once you start cooking, don't forget to taste your food—there's absolutely no other way to know if it needs more seasoning, herbs, or spices. But go easy, especially in the case of salt; remember, it's easy to add more but impossible to take it away. When serving hot food, warm the plates in the bottom of the oven, likewise the serving dishes if your guests are going to help themselves at the table. For specifics on carrying out certain techniques, such as cleaning fish, see Techniques in Detail, p. 95.

Armed with these basics, you'll soon be turning out food with the ease of a pro – antipasti of Tomato Bruschetta (p. 22) and Sweet-and-Sour Caponata (p. 16), classic pasta dishes such as Linguine with Pesto (p. 46), main courses like Spare Ribs with Polenta (p. 56), and irresistible desserts such as Raspberry Semifreddo (p. 75) and Tiramisu (p. 77), which are perfect for sharing with family and friends. You'll be able to create your very own *dolce vita*.

Buon appetito a tutti!

APPETIZERS

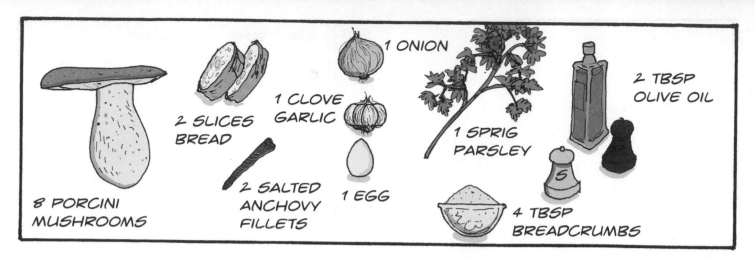

8 PORCINI MUSHROOMS

2 SLICES BREAD

1 CLOVE GARLIC

2 SALTED ANCHOVY FILLETS

1 ONION

1 EGG

1 SPRIG PARSLEY

4 TBSP BREADCRUMBS

2 TBSP OLIVE OIL

STUFFED PORCINI MUSHROOMS

SERVES 4 PREP: 40 MIN COOK: 20 MIN

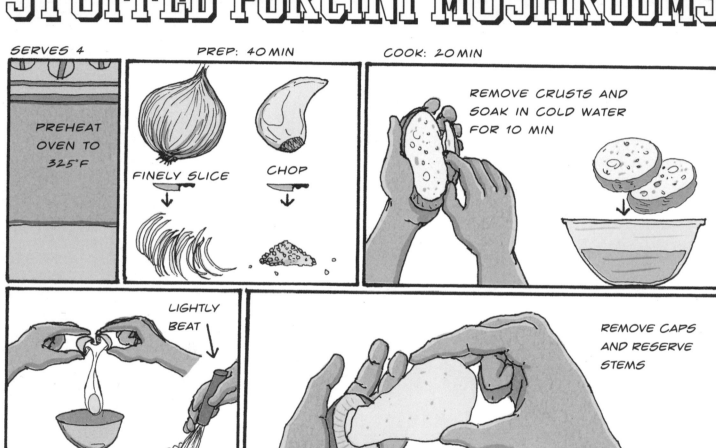

PREHEAT OVEN TO 325°F

FINELY SLICE

CHOP

REMOVE CRUSTS AND SOAK IN COLD WATER FOR 10 MIN

LIGHTLY BEAT

REMOVE CAPS AND RESERVE STEMS

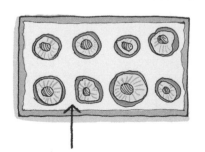

5 MIN IN OVEN THEN REMOVE

KEEP THE OVEN ON AND INCREASE HEAT TO 350°F

LINE A BAKING SHEET WITH WAX PAPER

TRANSFER CAPS TO A PLATE

DISCARD WAX PAPER

BRUSH SHEET WITH OIL

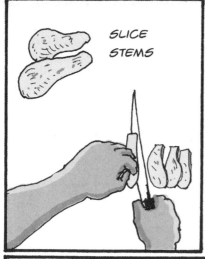

SLICE STEMS

CHOP ANCHOVIES

HEAT 1 TBSP OIL THEN COOK ONION

PARSLEY

ANCHOVIES AND GARLIC

LOW HEAT

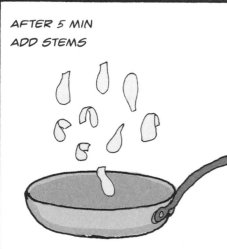

AFTER 5 MIN ADD STEMS

COOK FOR 3–4 MIN AND SEASON

THEN REMOVE FROM HEAT

SQUEEZE OUT THE BREAD

1 TBSP OIL, BREAD, AND EGG

AND MIX WELL

PLACE CAPS ON SHEET

FILL WITH MIXTURE

SPRINKLE WITH BREADCRUMBS

BAKE FOR 20 MIN

15

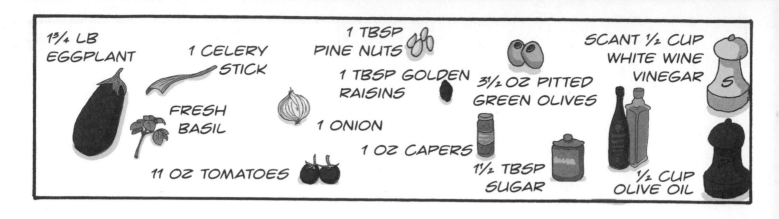

1¾ LB EGGPLANT

1 CELERY STICK

FRESH BASIL

11 OZ TOMATOES

1 TBSP PINE NUTS

1 TBSP GOLDEN RAISINS

1 ONION

1 OZ CAPERS

1½ TBSP SUGAR

3½ OZ PITTED GREEN OLIVES

SCANT ½ CUP WHITE WINE VINEGAR

½ CUP OLIVE OIL

SWEET-AND-SOUR CAPONATA

SERVES 4   PREP: 20 MIN   COOK: 20–25 MIN

TOAST PINE NUTS — LOW HEAT

DICE EGGPLANT

CHOP CELERY

SLICE ONION

BLANCH TOMATOES → BOILING WATER → ICE WATER → PEEL → CHOP

HEAT 5 TBSP OLIVE OIL

ADD EGGPLANT — STIR UNTIL GOLDEN BROWN — MEDIUM HEAT

meanwhile ... IN ANOTHER PAN...

HEAT THE REST OF THE OIL

CELERY   ONION   TOMATO — COOK FOR 10–15 MIN UNTIL THICK — LOW HEAT

STIR IN SUGAR, VINEGAR, PINE NUTS, CAPERS...

... GOLDEN RAISINS, AND OLIVES

BRING TO A BOIL, ADD THE EGGPLANT — AND SIMMER FOR 10 MIN — LOW HEAT

SERVE HOT OR WARM WITH BASIL

4 SQUID

1 SPRIG PARSLEY

½ CLOVE GARLIC

LEMON WEDGES

OLIVE OIL, FOR DRIZZLING AND BRUSHING

2 OZ BREADCRUMBS

BROILED STUFFED SQUID

SERVES 4   PREP: 30 MIN   COOK: 10 MIN

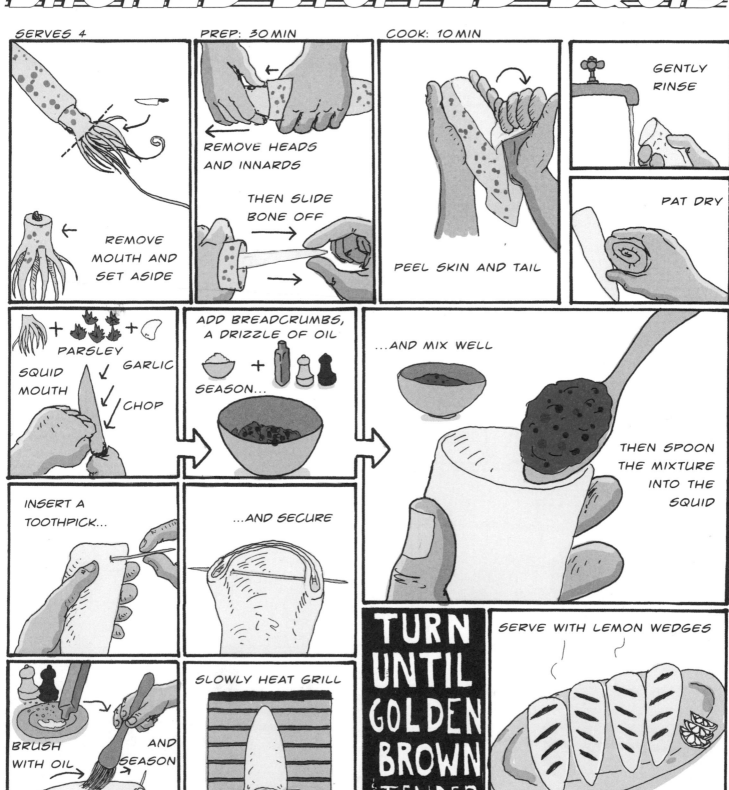

REMOVE MOUTH AND SET ASIDE

REMOVE HEADS AND INNARDS

THEN SLIDE BONE OFF

PEEL SKIN AND TAIL

GENTLY RINSE

PAT DRY

SQUID MOUTH + PARSLEY + GARLIC

CHOP

ADD BREADCRUMBS, A DRIZZLE OF OIL

SEASON...

...AND MIX WELL

THEN SPOON THE MIXTURE INTO THE SQUID

INSERT A TOOTHPICK...

...AND SECURE

BRUSH WITH OIL

AND SEASON

SLOWLY HEAT GRILL

TURN UNTIL GOLDEN BROWN & TENDER

SERVE WITH LEMON WEDGES

17

4 BELL PEPPERS

1 TOMATO

11 OZ CANNED TUNA

10 PITTED BLACK OLIVES

1 RED CHILE, CHOPPED

¾ TBSP LEMON JUICE

FRESH BASIL

1 TBSP OLIVE OIL

ROLLED PEPPERS

SERVES 4   PREP: 15 MIN   COOK: 10 MIN

GRILL BELL PEPPERS UNTIL CHARRED AND BLACKENED

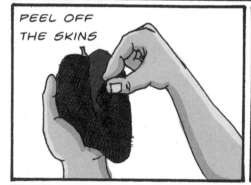

PLACE IN A PLASTIC BAG, TIE THE TOP, AND LEAVE TO COOL

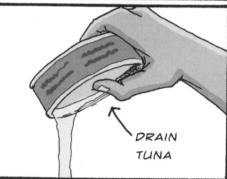

PEEL OFF THE SKINS

DRAIN TUNA

BLANCH TOMATOES

BOILING WATER

ICE WATER

PEEL

CHOP

SEED BELL PEPPERS

AND CUT INTO 2–3 LARGE SLICES

TUNA   TOMATOES   BASIL

OLIVES

CHILE

PROCESS

ADD LEMON JUICE AND OLIVE OIL

SPREAD ONTO PEPPER SLICES

ROLL UP

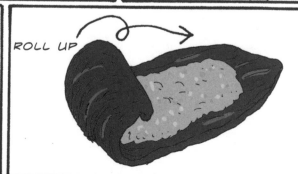

LET COOL BEFORE SERVING

18

4 SMALL SLICES
BACON FAT (LARDO)

4 EGGS

¼ CUP HEAVY
CREAM

2 TBSP
PARMESAN
(WHEN GRATED)

EGGS EN COCOTTE

SERVES 4   PREP: 10 MIN   COOK: 6–8 MIN

PREHEAT OVEN
TO 350°F

PARBOIL FOR
1 MIN

PUT
1 SLICE
BACON
FAT AND
1 TBSP
CREAM
IN EACH
RAMEKIN

PLACE RAMEKINS
IN ROASTING PAN

POUR IN
BOILING
WATER
TO HALF
WAY UP
RAMEKINS

Bake

FOR 6–8 MIN

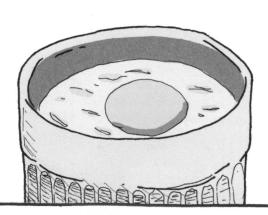

THE COMBINATION
OF STRONG AND
SAVORY BACON
FAT WITH THE MILD
TASTE OF CREAM
GIVES THE EGGS A
DELICATE FLAVOR

PIZZA MARGHERITA

SERVES 4   PREP: 1½ HR   COOK: 25 MIN

SIFT FLOUR AND PINCH SALT

MASH FRESH YEAST WITH THE WATER

MAKE A WELL IN THE FLOUR AND POUR IN THE YEAST MIXTURE

GENTLY STIR

UNTIL SOFT AND NOT TOO STICKY

AND ON A FLOURED SURFACE...

...KNEAD FOR 10 MIN

OR UNTIL SMOOTH AND ELASTIC

SHAPE INTO A BALL

COVER WITH OILED PLASTIC WRAP

LET RISE IN A WARM PLACE FOR 1 HR UNTIL DOUBLED IN SIZE

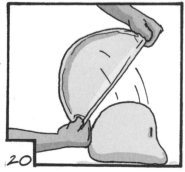

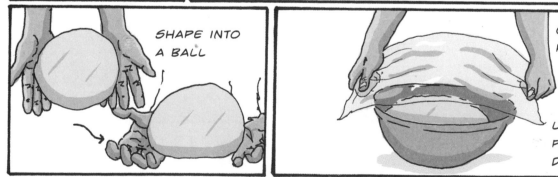

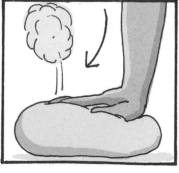

Margherita

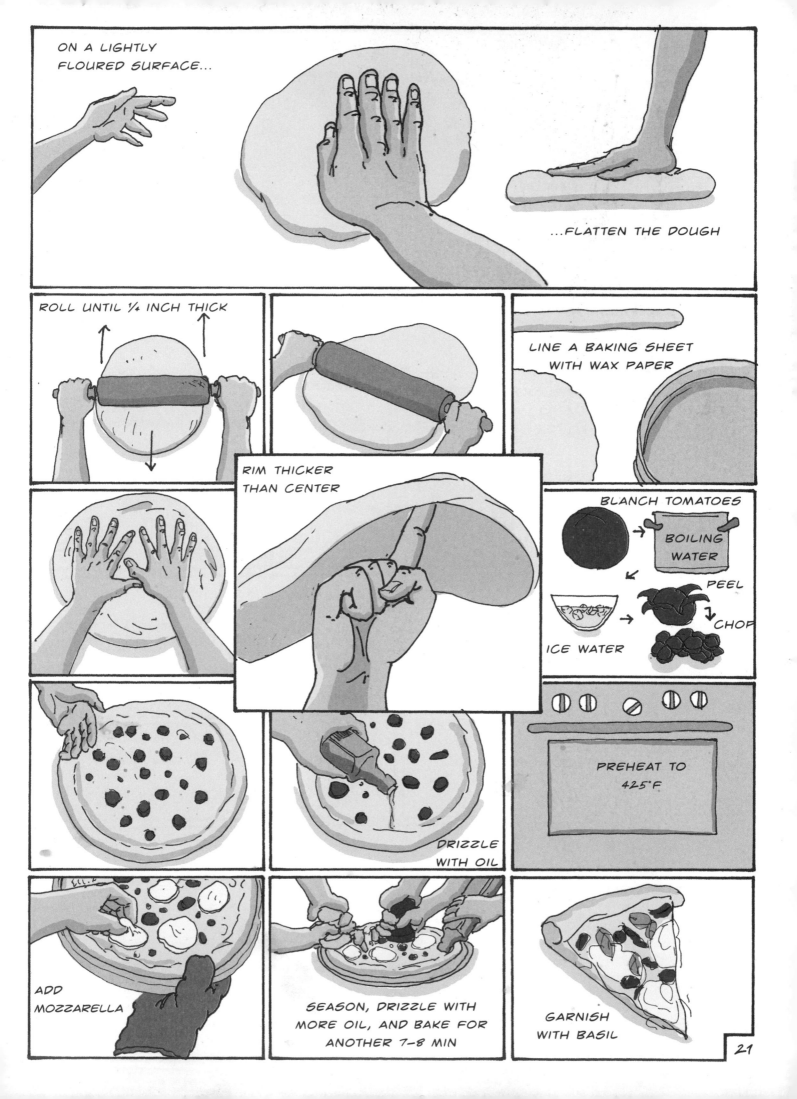

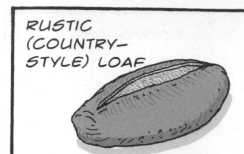 RUSTIC (COUNTRY-STYLE) LOAF

 4 GARLIC CLOVES

 6-8 PLUM TOMATOES

 EXTRA-VIRGIN OLIVE OIL

TOMATO BRUSCHETTA

SERVES 4   PREP: 20 MIN   COOKING: 5 MIN

Dice

 SLICE THE BREAD

 ↑ PREHEATED BROILER

TOAST ONE SIDE

THEN THE OTHER

 RUB WITH GARLIC WHILE STILL HOT

 PUT BACK UNDER THE BROILER FOR A MOMENT

 TOP WITH TOMATOES

 SEASON

AND DRIZZLE WITH OIL

 SERVE

 ALTERNATIVE BRUSCHETTA TOPPINGS ARE:

MOZZARELLA, PROSCIUTTO, ANCHOVIES, FAVA BEANS, BASIL

1¾ LB FLOURY POTATOES

3½ OZ FONTINA CHEESE

2 OZ COOKED HAM

1 SPRIG BASIL

3 EGGS

VEGETABLE OIL

2 OZ PARMESAN

3 OZ BREADCRUMBS

POTATO CROQUETTES

SERVES 4   PREP: 1½ HR   30–40 MIN

COOK FOR 45 MIN

SALTED BOILING WATER

GRATE PARMESAN

HAM

CUT INTO STICKS

FONTINA

PEEL AND MASH THE POTATOES

ADD 1 EGG AND 1 YOLK TO THE POTATOES

THEN ADD PARMESAN, SEASON AND MIX

SHAPE

PUSH A STICK OF HAM AND FONTINA INTO EACH CROQUETTE

BEATEN EGG

BREADCRUMBS

HEAT OIL IN A DEEP PAN TO 350°F OR UNTIL A CUBE OF BREAD BROWNS IN 30 SEC AND FRY CROQUETTES UNTIL GOLDEN

GARNISH WITH BASIL

23

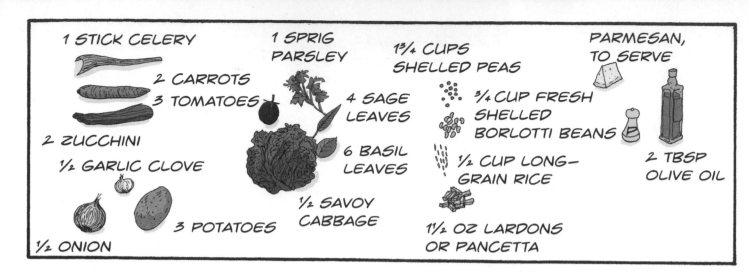

MILANESE MINESTRONE

SERVES 4–6 　　　PREP: 30 MIN 　　　COOK: 2½ HR

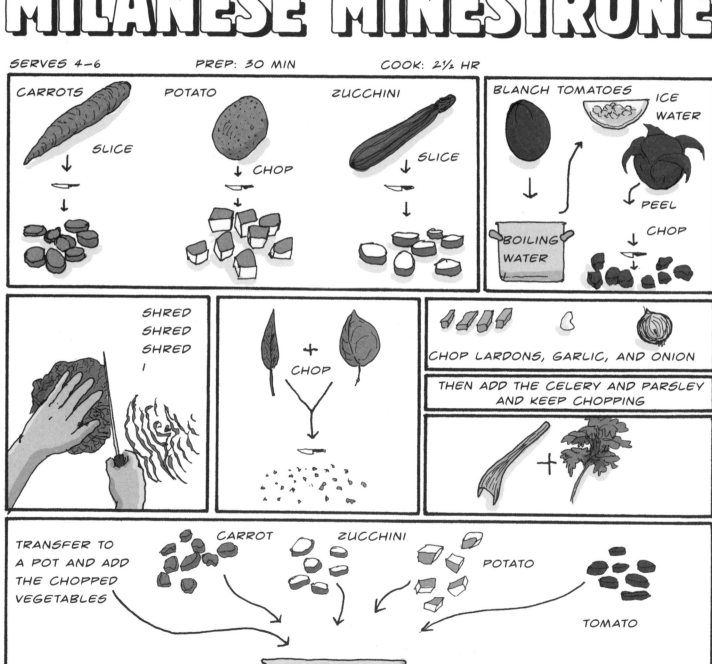

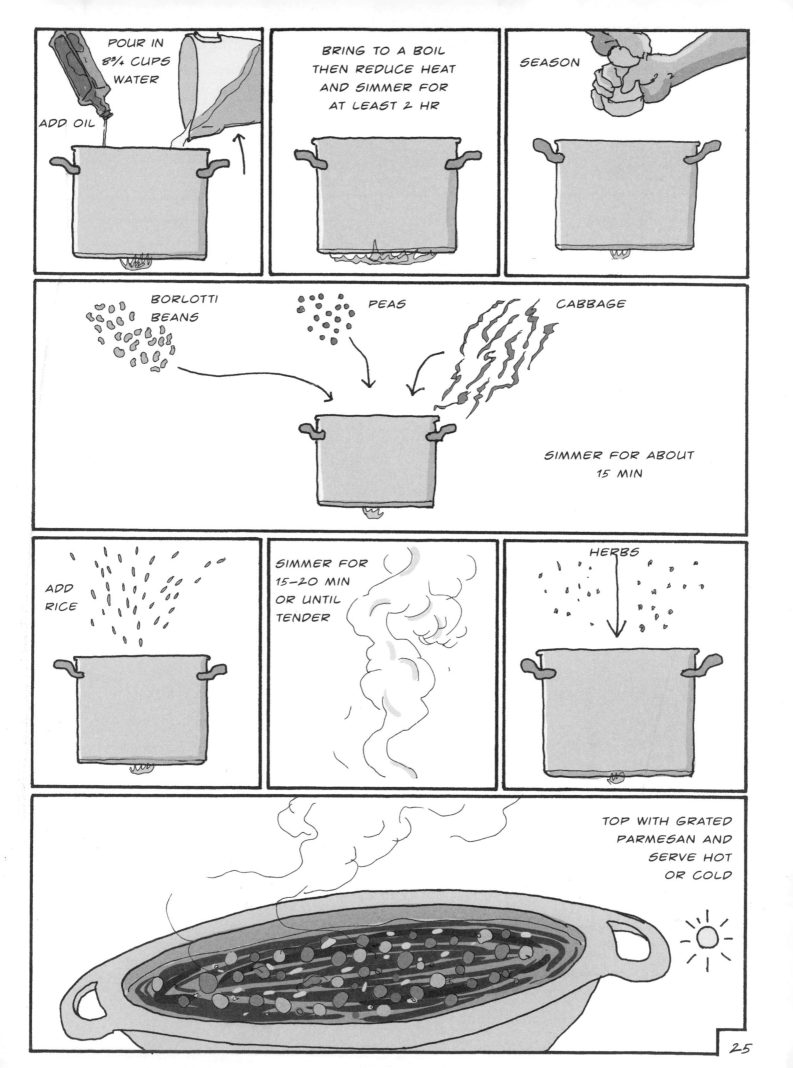

4½ CUPS ALL-PURPOSE FLOUR

 1 OZ FRESH YEAST

 9 OZ RICOTTA

 5 OZ COOKED HAM

 4–5 FIRM RED CHERRY TOMATOES

 OLIVE OIL, FOR DEEP-FRYING

PANZAROTTI

SERVES 4   PREP: 3¾ HR   COOK: 8–10 MIN

 SIFT FLOUR
+ PINCH SALT
INTO A MOUND

MASH FRESH YEAST WITH 1 CUP LUKEWARM WATER

THEN POUR INTO WELL

WELL

INCORPORATE INTO FLOUR UNTIL A DOUGH FORMS

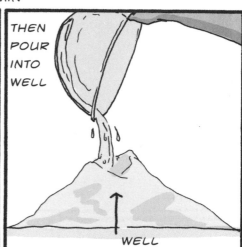 KNEAD DOUGH UNTIL SMOOTH AND ELASTIC

 SHAPE INTO A BALL THEN PLACE IN A BOWL

COVER WITH A DISH TOWEL LET RISE IN A WARM PLACE FOR 2–3 HR UNTIL DOUBLED IN SIZE
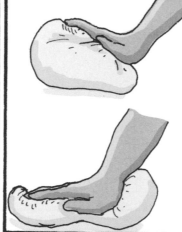
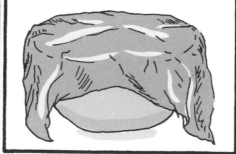

BLANCH TOMATOES
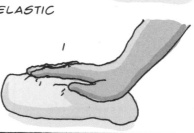 BOILING WATER → ICE WATER
PEEL
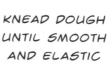
CHOP

DICE HAM

MIX RICOTTA AND HAM AND SEASON

DIVIDE DOUGH INTO 8 EQUAL PORTIONS

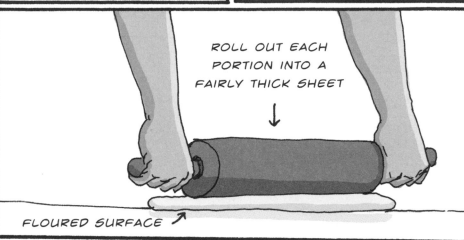

ROLL OUT EACH PORTION INTO A FAIRLY THICK SHEET

FLOURED SURFACE ↗

SPOON THE RICOTTA MIXTURE ONTO THE DOUGH SHEETS

TOP WITH TOMATOES

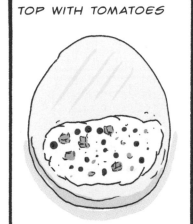

FOLD DOUGH OVER FILLING AND CRIMP EDGES WITH A FORK TO SEAL

HEAT OIL IN A DEEP-FRYER TO 350°F OR UNTIL...

...A CUBE OF BREAD BROWNS IN 30 SEC

ADD PANZAROTTI AND COOK FOR 8–10 MIN UNTIL GOLDEN

REMOVE WITH A SLOTTED SPOON, DRAIN ON PAPER TOWELS, AND SERVE

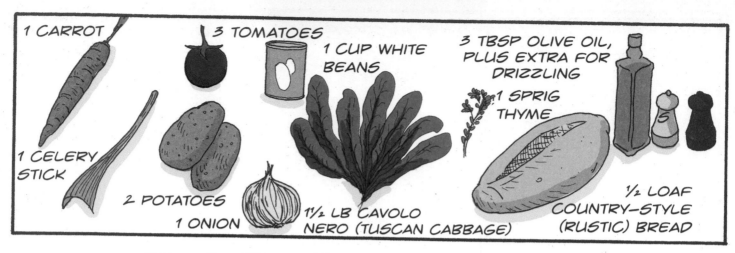

RIBOLLITA

SERVES 4   PREP: 30 MIN   COOK: 2½ HR

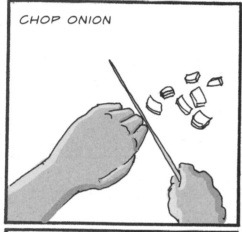

CHOP ONION

CHOP CARROT

CHOP CELERY

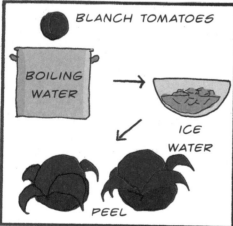

BLANCH TOMATOES

BOILING WATER → ICE WATER

PEEL

PEEL AND DICE POTATOES

SHRED CAVOLO NERO

HEAT OIL

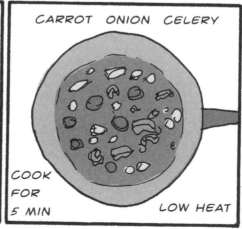

CARROT ONION CELERY

COOK FOR 5 MIN   LOW HEAT

ADD TOMATOES, THYME, AND POTATOES

COOK FOR A FEW MIN...

8 SLICES RUSTIC (COUNTRY-STYLE) WHITE BREAD

8 BASIL LEAVES

EXTRA-VIRGIN OLIVE OIL, FOR DRIZZLING

4 FIRM RED TOMATOES

PANZANELLA

SERVES 4   PREP: 10 MIN

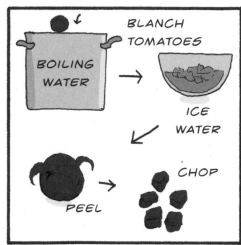

BLANCH TOMATOES

BOILING WATER

ICE WATER

PEEL → CHOP

REMOVE BREAD CRUSTS AND SOAK THE BREAD IN A BOWL OF COLD WATER FOR A FEW MIN

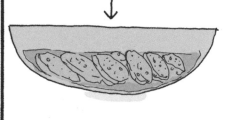

SQUEEZE OUT BREAD

AND PLACE IN A LARGE SALAD BOWL

SEASON THE BREAD

SPRINKLE WITH BASIL

DRIZZLE GENEROUSLY WITH OIL

RIP THE BREAD WITH TWO FORKS TO BREAK IT UP

ADD THE TOMATOES...

...AND SERVE

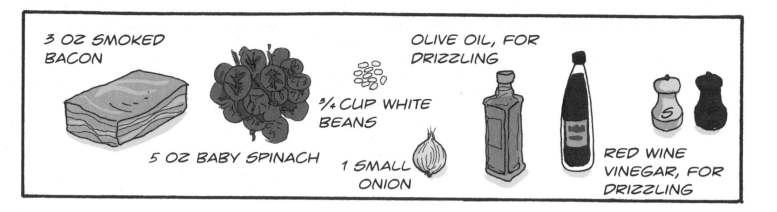

SPINACH SALAD WITH BACON & BEANS

SERVES 4   PREP: 10 MIN   COOK: 5 MIN

SOAK BEANS OVERNIGHT *Boil* UNTIL TENDER AND THEN DRAIN

PREHEAT THE BROILER

LINE BAKING SHEET WITH WAX PAPER

CHOP BACON   SLICE ONION

SPRINKLE BACON ONTO LINED SHEET

BROIL BACON FOR 5 MIN UNTIL CRISP

ADD OIL AND VINEGAR + SEASON

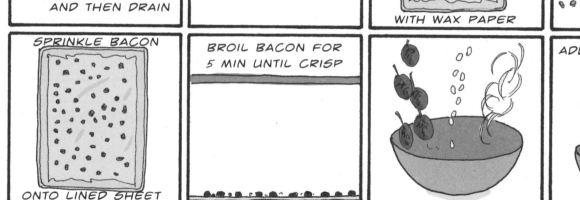

GENTLY TOSS THE SALAD

BUON APPETITO

SPRINKLE THE SALAD WITH BACON

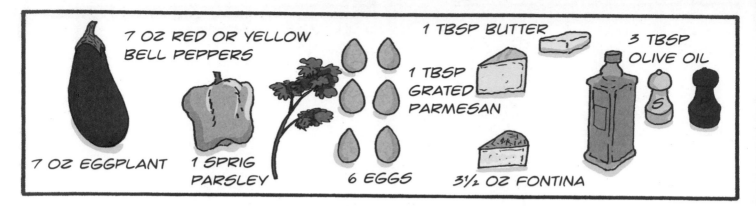

7 OZ RED OR YELLOW BELL PEPPERS

7 OZ EGGPLANT

1 SPRIG PARSLEY

6 EGGS

1 TBSP BUTTER

1 TBSP GRATED PARMESAN

3½ OZ FONTINA

3 TBSP OLIVE OIL

FRITTATA CAKE

SERVES 6   PREP: 30 MIN   COOK: 30 MIN

PREHEAT BROILER

SLICE THE EGGPLANT AND BROIL UNTIL GOLDEN

CHOP PARSLEY

BROIL BELL PEPPERS UNTIL BLACKENED AND CHARRED

TRANSFER TO A PLASTIC FOOD BAG AND SEAL THE TOP

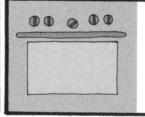

PREHEAT OVEN TO 475°F

PEEL

SEED

CUT INTO STRIPS

2 EGGS   IN SEPARATE BOWLS BEAT

2 EGGS

BOWL 1

BOWL 2

DIVIDE PARSLEY BETWEEN THE 2 BOWLS AND SEASON

BOWL 1

BOWL 2

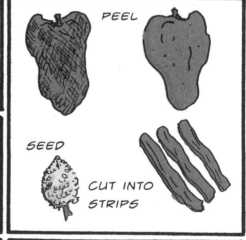

BEAT 2 EGGS AND PARMESAN AND SEASON

BOWL 3

HEAT 1 TBSP OLIVE OIL + THE BUTTER

POUR IN CONTENTS OF BOWL 1, COOK UNTIL SET ON ONE SIDE BUT STILL SOFT ON THE OTHER

THEN CAREFULLY SLIDE THE FRITTATA ONTO A PLATE

COOK

THE CONTENTS OF THE OTHER 2 BOWLS IN THE SAME WAY

LINE A CAKE PAN WITH WAX PAPER

SLICE THE FONTINA

PLACE ONE PARSLEY FRITTATA IN THE TIN

SOFT SIDE UP

COVER WITH THE EGGPLANT AND HALF THE FONTINA

PLACE PARMESAN FRITTATA ON TOP, SOFT SIDE UP

TOP WITH BELL PEPPER STRIPS AND REMAINING FONTINA

TOP WITH SECOND PARSLEY FRITTATA

SOFT SIDE DOWN

BAKE

FOR 10 MIN

SERVE HOT OR COLD

33

1 CARROT

11 OZ GROUND MEAT

1 ONION

SCANT ½ CUP DRY WHITE WINE OR WATER

FRESH NUTMEG

1 CUP PASSATA

2½ OZ PARMESAN

⅔ STICK BUTTER, PLUS EXTRA FOR GREASING

GENEROUS 2 CUPS MILK

¼ CUP ALL-PURPOSE FLOUR

1 QUANTITY FRESH PASTA (SEE P. 44), CUT INTO 4-INCH SQUARES

3 TBSP OLIVE OIL

LASAGNA BOLOGNESE

SERVES 4   PREP: 2 HR 50 MIN   COOK: 30 MIN

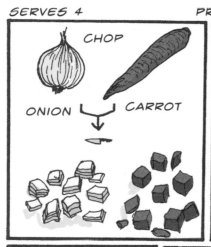
CHOP
ONION   CARROT

LOW HEAT

AFTER 5 MIN ADD THE MEAT

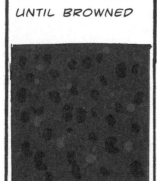
COOK THE MEAT UNTIL BROWNED

POUR IN WINE

LET WINE EVAPORATE, SEASON AND ADD PASSATA

12
6
SIMMER FOR 30 MIN AND THEN CHECK SEASONING

PREHEAT OVEN TO 210°F

Béchamel

MELT ½ STICK BUTTER
LOW HEAT

WHISK IN FLOUR

SLOWLY POUR IN MILK

WHISK CONSTANTLY UNTIL SMOOTH

BRING TO A BOIL, STIRRING CONSTANTLY

COVER

SIMMER FOR 20 MIN, STIRRING OCCASIONALLY

SEASON

ADD PINCH GRATED NUTMEG

GREASE OVENPROOF DISH WITH BUTTER

COOK PASTA UNTIL AL DENTE, THEN DRAIN

SALTED BOILING WATER

LAY PASTA IN BOTTOM OF DISH

ADD LAYER OF BOTH SAUCES

DOT WITH BUTTER

AND SPRINKLE WITH PARMESAN

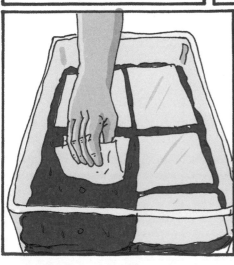

REPEAT LAYERS UNTIL PASTA AND SAUCES ALL USED

BAKE FOR 30 MIN

TAGLIATELLE WITH PEAS & HAM

SERVES 4   PREP: 15 MIN   COOK: 35 MIN

1½ LB SPINACH

2 EGG YOLKS

2 OZ PARMESAN

1¾ CUPS ALL-PURPOSE FLOUR

1¾ LB POTATOES

½ STICK BUTTER, MELTED

POTATO & SPINACH GNOCCHI

SERVES 4   PREP: 40 MIN   COOK: 25–30 MIN

Peel BOIL MASH

WASH, DRAIN, AND COOK FOR 3–5 MIN

SQUEEZE SPINACH
THEN CHOP

MASH
MIX

SEASON
ADD EGG YOLKS
TO POTATO AND SPINACH

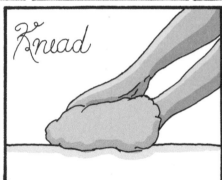
Knead

DON'T KNEAD TOO MUCH

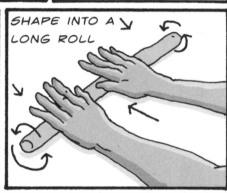
SHAPE INTO A LONG ROLL

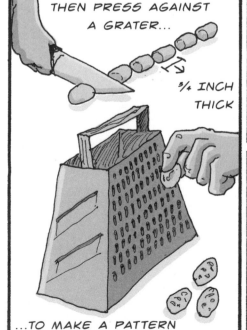
CUT INTO PIECES THEN PRESS AGAINST A GRATER...
¾ INCH THICK
...TO MAKE A PATTERN

DUST WITH FLOUR

SALTED BOILING WATER
BOIL, THEN REMOVE GNOCCHI WHEN THEY RISE TO SURFACE

MIX IN MELTED BUTTER AND GRATED PARMESAN

AND SERVE

FUSILLI WITH MUSHROOMS

SERVES 4   PREP: 20 MIN   COOK: 1 HR

CHOP ONION

SLICE AND CHOP MUSHROOMS

HEAT OIL

ADD TOMATOES AND SEASON

SIMMER FOR 45 MIN, REMOVE FROM HEAT AND ADD PARSLEY

BOIL FUSILLI

THEN DRAIN

SALTED BOILING WATER

ADD PARMESAN AND BUTTER TO FUSILLI AND TOSS

SERVE

12 OZ SPAGHETTI

2 EGGS

1½ OZ PARMESAN

¼ STICK BUTTER

1 GARLIC CLOVE

1½ OZ PECORINO CHEESE

3½ OZ PANCETTA

SPAGHETTI CARBONARA

SERVES 4

PREP: 15 MIN

COOK: 20 MIN

GRATE BOTH CHEESES

DICE PANCETTA

ADD PANCETTA AND GARLIC CLOVE

MELT BUTTER. REMOVE CLOVE... ...WHEN GOLDEN

MEANWHILE... COOK THE PASTA

SALTED BOILING WATER

al dente.

LIGHTLY BEAT THE EGGS

DRAIN PASTA

RESERVE SOME COOKING WATER

ADD PASTA TO PANCETTA AND BUTTER

ADD A LITTLE COOKING WATER

ADD EGG AND SEASON

ADD HALF THE CHEESE AND...

TOSS

UNTIL THE EGG COATS THE PASTA

SPRINKLE WITH REMAINING CHEESE

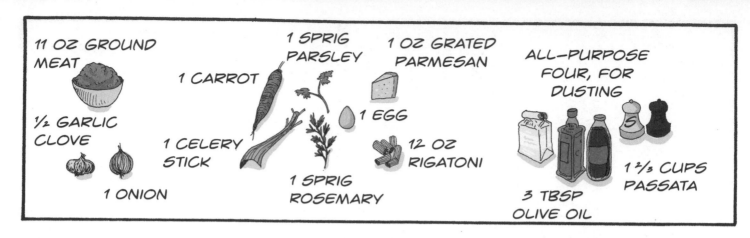

RIGATONI WITH MEATBALLS

SERVES 4   PREP: 20 MIN   COOK: 1 HR

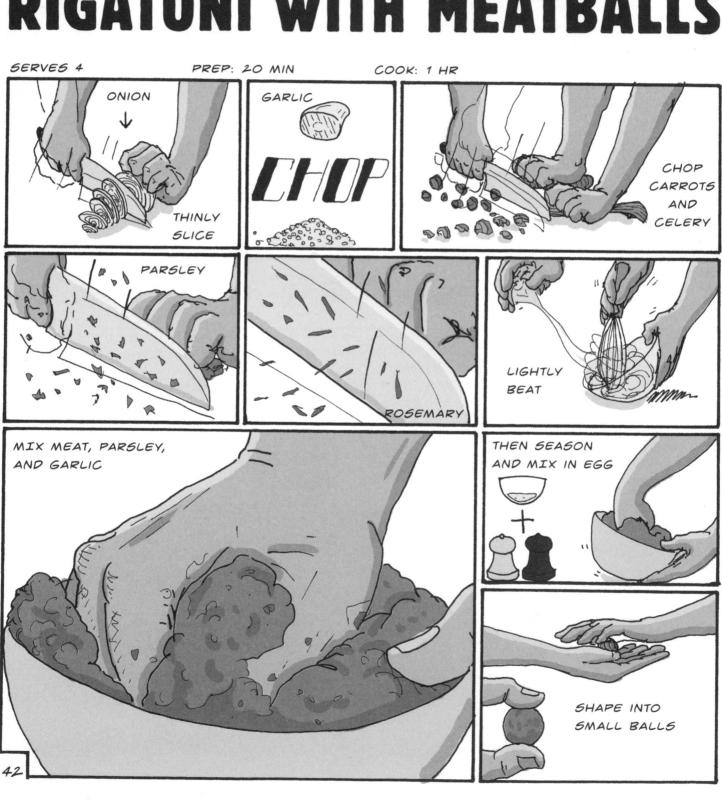

ONION → THINLY SLICE

GARLIC CHOP

CHOP CARROTS AND CELERY

PARSLEY

ROSEMARY

LIGHTLY BEAT

MIX MEAT, PARSLEY, AND GARLIC

THEN SEASON AND MIX IN EGG

SHAPE INTO SMALL BALLS

42

DUST WITH FLOUR

HEAT

OLIVE OIL

LOW HEAT

ONION   CARROT   CELERY   ROSEMARY

COOK FOR 5 MIN

LOW HEAT

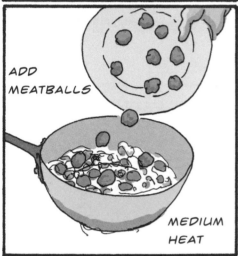

ADD MEATBALLS

MEDIUM HEAT

COOK UNTIL LIGHTLY BROWNED ALL OVER

SEASON AND ADD PASSATA

SIMMER FOR 40 MIN

STIRRING OCCASIONALLY

SALTED BOILING WATER

DRAIN

ADD TO PAN AND COOK FOR 2 MIN

TOP WITH PARMESAN

DELIZIOSO!

8 FRESH
SAGE
LEAVES

½ STICK
BUTTER

3 EGGS

2¾ CUPS
ALL-PURPOSE
FLOUR

2 OZ PARMESAN, PLUS
2 TBSP GRATED
PARMESAN

3¼ LB SPINACH

2¾ CUPS RICOTTA

VEGETABLE- & CHEESE-FILLED RAVIOLI

SERVES 6   PREP: 2 HR   COOK: 10 MIN

PASTA

FILLING

SIFT FLOUR AND PINCH SALT

MAKE A WELL

WASH, DRAIN, AND COOK SPINACH FOR 5 MIN

BEAT 2 EGGS AND 1 YOLK

POUR EGGS IN THE WELL

CHOP SPINACH

KNEAD

INCORPORATE EGGS INTO FLOUR

UNTIL SMOOTH THEN REST FOR 1 HR

MIX THE SPINACH WITH...

...2¼ CUPS RICOTTA

ADD 2 EGGS

AND 2 TBSP PARMESAN

Stir

UNTIL VERY SMOOTH

ROLL OUT PASTA AND LET DRY

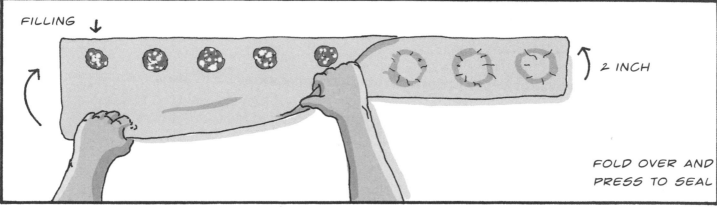

FILLING ↓

↑ 2 INCH

FOLD OVER AND PRESS TO SEAL

CUT INTO SQUARES

MELT BUTTER AND COOK SAGE UNTIL GOLDEN

LOW HEAT

COOK RAVIOLI & DRAIN

MIND THE FRESH PASTA COOKING TIME: ONLY 1–2 MIN!

CRUMBLE OVER

½ CUP RICOTTA AND THE GRATED PARMESAN

POUR OVER THE BUTTER AND SAGE

AND SERVE

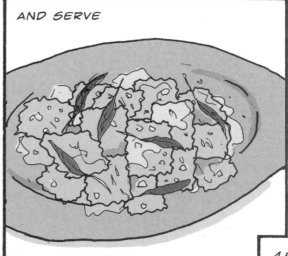

45

2 GARLIC CLOVES
1 OZ PECORINO
2 POTATOES
12 OZ LINGUINE
5 TBSP OLIVE OIL
25 BASIL LEAVES
1 OZ PARMESAN
2 OZ GREEN BEANS

LINGUINE WITH PESTO

SERVES 4   PREP: 30 MIN   COOK: 12-15 MIN

GRATE PECORINO AND PARMESAN

BASIL
GARLIC
CHOP
OIL AND SEASON
BLITZ IN A FOOD PROCESSOR UNTIL SMOOTH

ADD CHEESES

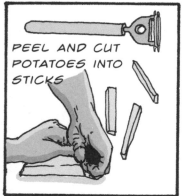

PEEL AND CUT POTATOES INTO STICKS

BOIL POTATO STICKS AND LINGUINE FOR 10 MIN THEN ADD THE BEANS...

SALTED BOILING WATER

...AND BOIL FOR ANOTHER 5 MIN OR UNTIL PASTA IS AL DENTE

DRAIN

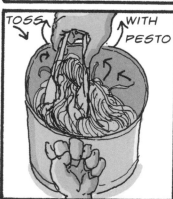

TOSS WITH PESTO

AND SERVE

ALTERNATIVELY, USE A PESTLE AND MORTAR TO MAKE THE PESTO

GRIND UNTIL SMOOTH

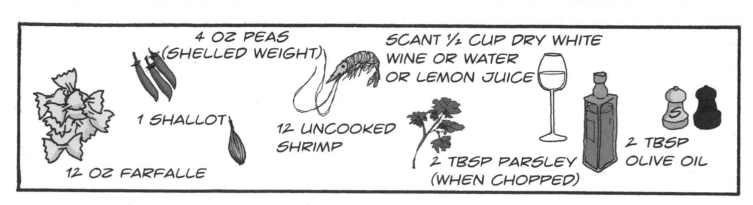

4 OZ PEAS
(SHELLED WEIGHT)

1 SHALLOT

12 OZ FARFALLE

12 UNCOOKED
SHRIMP

SCANT ½ CUP DRY WHITE
WINE OR WATER
OR LEMON JUICE

2 TBSP PARSLEY
(WHEN CHOPPED)

2 TBSP
OLIVE OIL

FARFALLE WITH SHRIMP

SERVES 4   PREP: 20 MIN   COOK: 30 MIN

SHELL
PEAS

CHOP
SHALLOT

MAKE A SURFACE
INCISION

PEEL
SHRIMP

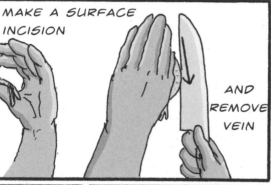

AND
REMOVE
VEIN

CHOP
PARSLEY

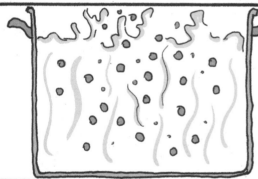

BLANCH
PEAS FOR
5 MIN IN
SALTED
BOILING
WATER
THEN
DRAIN

HEAT OLIVE
OIL

SHALLOT

LOW
HEAT

ADD PEAS AND...

...COOK FOR 10 MIN

ADD SHRIMP AND
WINE AND COOK
UNTIL LIQUID
EVAPORATES

THEN
COOK
FOR 3 MIN

MEANWHILE COOK THE PASTA
UNTIL AL DENTE

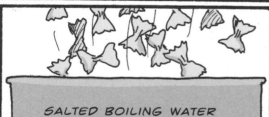

SALTED BOILING WATER

DRAIN PASTA AND TIP INTO PAN
WITH SAUCE

AND TOSS
OVER HEAT
FOR 2 MIN

SEASON WITH PEPPER

SPRINKLE WITH PARSLEY AND
SERVE

47

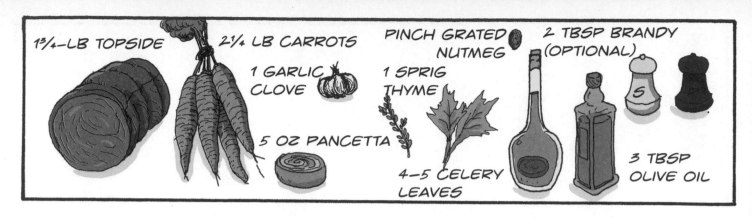

Ingredients

1¾-LB TOPSIDE

2¼ LB CARROTS

1 GARLIC CLOVE

5 OZ PANCETTA

PINCH GRATED NUTMEG

1 SPRIG THYME

4-5 CELERY LEAVES

2 TBSP BRANDY (OPTIONAL)

3 TBSP OLIVE OIL

ROAST BEEF WITH CARROTS

SERVES 6   PREP: 20 MIN   COOK: 2½ HR

PREHEAT OVEN TO 250°F

SLICE THE CARROTS

THYME + GARLIC
CHOP CHOP CHOP

CHOP PANCETTA

SPRINKLE TWO-THIRDS INTO A ROASTING PAN

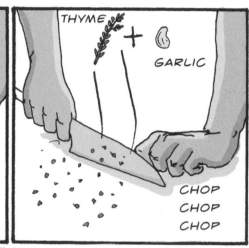
HEAT THE OIL THEN COOK CARROTS, GARLIC, AND THYME
MEDIUM HEAT

SEASON AND ADD NUTMEG

KEEP WARM

TIE THE MEAT WITH STRING

ADD TO THE EMPTIED PAN AND COOK

TURNING FREQUENTLY UNTIL BROWN

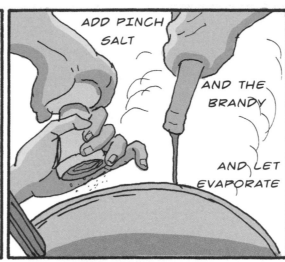

ADD PINCH SALT

AND THE BRANDY

AND LET EVAPORATE

YOU CAN USE WATER OR STOCK INSTEAD IF YOU LIKE

TRANSFER TO THE ROASTING PAN

ADD CARROTS + CELERY LEAVES

SPRINKLE WITH REMAINING PANCETTA

COVER WITH FOIL

ROAST FOR 2 HR UNTIL CARROTS ARE CARAMELIZED

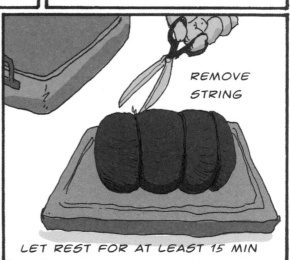

REMOVE STRING

LET REST FOR AT LEAST 15 MIN

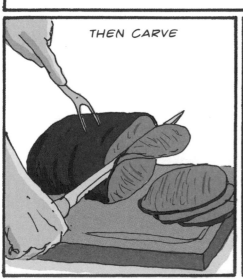

THEN CARVE

TRANSFER TO A WARM SERVING DISH

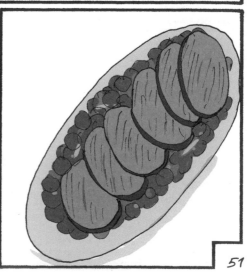

4 RUMP STEAKS

1 LB 5 OZ TOMATOES

2 GARLIC CLOVES

¼ STICK BUTTER

PINCH DRIED OREGANO

2 TBSP OLIVE OIL

STEAK PIZZAIOLA

SERVES 4   PREP: 30 MIN   COOK: 10 MIN

BLANCH TOMATOES

BOILING WATER → ICE WATER
PEEL
CHOP

OIL   BUTTER   WHEN HOT ADD GARLIC, FRY UNTIL BROWN, THEN REMOVE AND DISCARD

COOK 1 MINUTE EACH SIDE

KEEP WARM

TOMATO   OREGANO

COOK UNTIL THICKENED AND PULPY

RETURN TO THE PAN

AND COOK TO YOUR LIKING

RARE   MEDIUM   WELL DONE

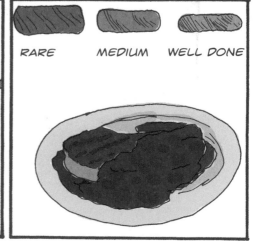

3¼ LB
MUSSELS

1 SPRIG
PARSLEY

BE SURE TO BUY
THE FRESHEST
MUSSELS

MUSSELS MARINARA

SERVES 4   PREP: 25 MIN   COOK: 5 MIN

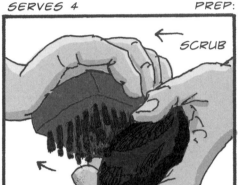

SCRUB

SCRUB

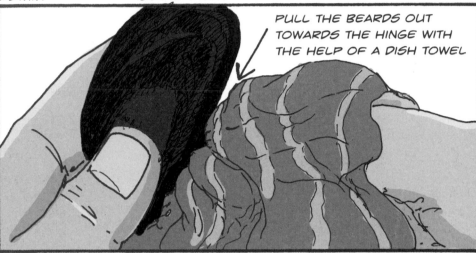

PULL THE BEARDS OUT
TOWARDS THE HINGE WITH
THE HELP OF A DISH TOWEL

SEASON
WITH PEPPER

NO WATER

HIGH HEAT

COOK FOR ABOUT
5 MIN UNTIL THE
SHELLS OPEN AND

DISCARD

ANY THAT REMAIN
CLOSED

DRAIN THE
COOKING
LIQUID INTO
A BOWL

STRAIN THROUGH
A FINE-MESH
STRAINER

CHOP PARSLEY
AND ADD TO THE
COOKING LIQUID

POUR LIQUID
OVER THE
MUSSELS

AND SERVE

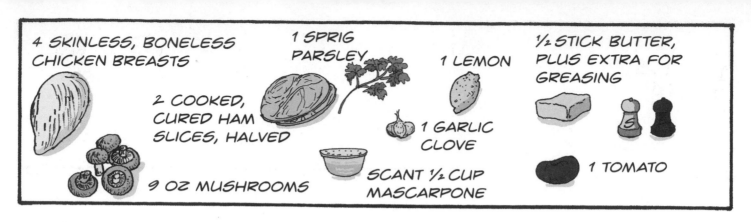

4 SKINLESS, BONELESS CHICKEN BREASTS

2 COOKED, CURED HAM SLICES, HALVED

9 OZ MUSHROOMS

1 SPRIG PARSLEY

1 GARLIC CLOVE

SCANT ½ CUP MASCARPONE

1 LEMON

½ STICK BUTTER, PLUS EXTRA FOR GREASING

1 TOMATO

CHICKEN STUFFED WITH MASCARPONE

SERVES 4   PREP: 50 MIN   COOK: 30 MIN

PREHEAT OVEN TO 400°F

GREASE A ROASTING PAN WITH BUTTER

CHOP MUSHROOMS

SQUEEZE LEMON

CHOP PARSLEY

MELT HALF THE BUTTER

LOW HEAT

ADD GARLIC AND REMOVE AND DISCARD WHEN BROWN

MUSHROOMS

PARSLEY

HIGH HEAT

COOK FOR 5 MIN THEN...

...REMOVE FROM HEAT AND SEASON

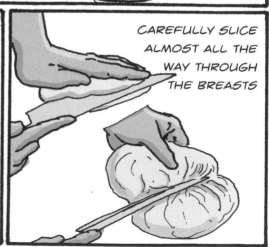

CAREFULLY SLICE ALMOST ALL THE WAY THROUGH THE BREASTS

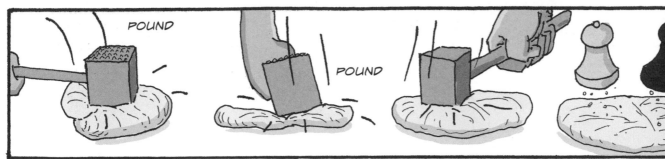

POUND POUND

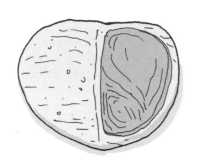

PLACE HALF SLICE OF HAM

SPREAD QUARTER OF THE MASCARPONE

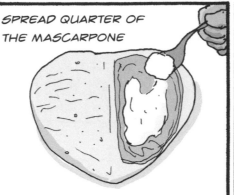

TOP WITH 1 TBSP MUSHROOMS

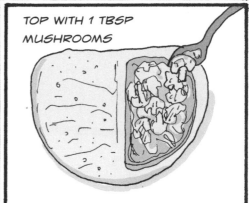

Fold CLOSED LIKE A BOOK

SECURE WITH TOOTHPICKS

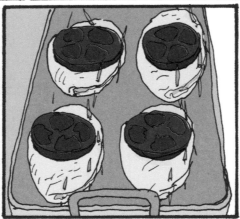

CUT THE TOMATO INTO SLICES

TOP WITH SLICES OF TOMATO

SEASON AND DOT WITH REMAINING BUTTER

ROAST

COVER WITH FOIL
ROAST FOR 15 MIN

MEANWHILE,
PREHEAT BROILER

REMOVE FOIL AND BROIL UNTIL GOLDEN BROWN

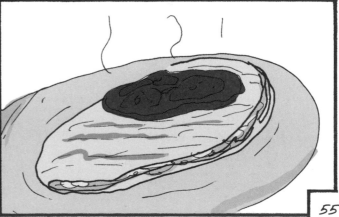

1¾ LB PORK SPARE RIBS

1 GARLIC CLOVE

¼ STICK BUTTER

¾ CUP RED WINE OR WARM WATER

1 FRESH CHILE

1 ONION

14 OZ CANNED TOMATOES

6 BASIL LEAVES, CHOPPED

3⅔ CUPS POLENTA FLOUR

SPARE RIBS WITH POLENTA

SERVES 4   PREP: 1½ HR   COOK: 1½ HR

CHILE

ONION

CHOP CHOP CHOP

MELT

ADD ONION, GARLIC, AND CHILE AND COOK FOR 10 MIN UNTIL GOLDEN BROWN

THEN REMOVE AND DISCARD GARLIC

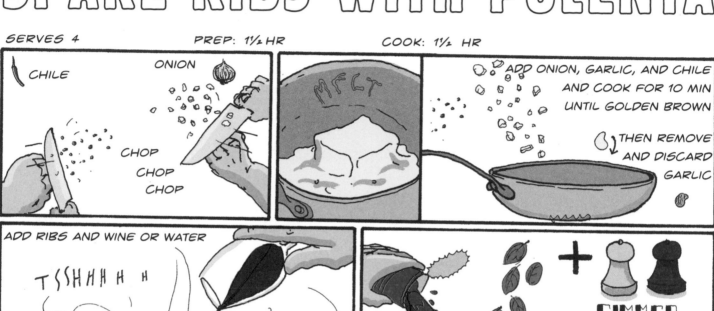

ADD RIBS AND WINE OR WATER

TSSHHH H

AND COOK...

UNTIL EVAPORATED

+ SIMMER FOR ABOUT 1 HR

ADD MORE WINE OR WATER IF NECESSARY

MEANWHILE MAKE THE

POLENTA

STIR THE POLENTA INTO 7½ CUPS SALTED BOILING WATER

COOK FOR ABOUT 45 MIN STIRRING CONTINUOUSLY UNTIL THICK

ADD A LITTLE HOT WATER TO SOFTEN

¼ STICK BUTTER

 6 SAGE LEAVES

4 PORK LOIN CHOPS, TRIMMED OF BONES

PORK CHOPS WITH BUTTER & SAGE

SERVES 4   PREP: 10 MIN   COOK: 15 MIN

BASH
WITH A MEAT MALLET

MELT THE BUTTER AND THEN ADD THE SAGE

LOW HEAT

DON'T BURN

THE BUTTER...

...OR THE SAGE

ADD THE MEAT AND COOK FOR ABOUT 5 MIN ON EACH SIDE...

...UNTIL TENDER AND COOKED THROUGH, THEN SEASON

SERVE WITH ROASTED OR MASHED POTATOES

AND SAVOY CABBAGE, BROCCOLI, OR GREEN BEANS

57

GRILLED SARDINES

1¾ LB SARDINES

½ RED CHILE

½ GARLIC CLOVE

JUICE OF 1 LEMON

1 TSP WORCESTERSHIRE SAUCE

5 TBSP OLIVE OIL

SERVES 4   PREP: 25 MIN   COOK: 4–5 MIN

DESCALE SARDINES

SLIDE KNIFE LENGTH OF BELLY, THEN RINSE

SNIP BONE HERE — REMOVE BONE

GARLIC, CHILE, LEMON JUICE, OIL, AND SAUCE

REMOVE HEAD

SLIDE THUMB TO THE TAIL

REMOVE ANY PIN BONES WITH A KNIFE OR TWEEZERS

BRUSH WITH OIL

CUT BELLY

SLIDE THUMB ON ONE SIDE

meanwhile HEAT THE BROILER

CHOP GARLIC

BROIL 2–3 MIN ON EACH SIDE

REMOVE GUTS AND DISCARD

...THEN THE OTHER

SEED AND CHOP CHILE

SERVE WITH THE SAUCE ON SIDE

1 ONION

1 CELERY STALK, PLUS A FEW LEAVES

4 HAKE STEAKS

1 SPRIG PARSLEY

JUICE OF 1 LEMON

2 TBSP OLIVE OIL, PLUS EXTRA FOR BRUSHING

HAKE IN GREEN SAUCE

SERVES 4   PREP: 15 MIN   COOK: 10 MIN

PREHEAT OVEN TO 400°F

ONION

CELERY

PARSLEY

CHOP CHOP CHOP

CHOP CHOP CHOP

CHOP CHOP CHOP

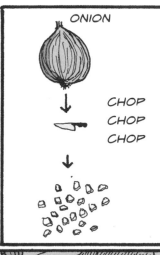

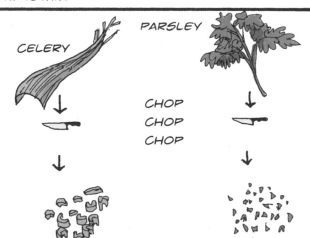

BRUSH OVENPROOF DISH WITH OIL

COOK STEAKS FOR 10 MIN MEANWHILE, MAKE THE SAUCE...

HEAT 2 TBSP OLIVE OIL

COOK ONION FOR 5 MIN UNTIL SOFT

→ LOW HEAT

SEASON

THEN REMOVE FROM THE HEAT

PARSLEY

CELERY

LEMON JUICE

POUR SAUCE OVER HAKE AND SERVE

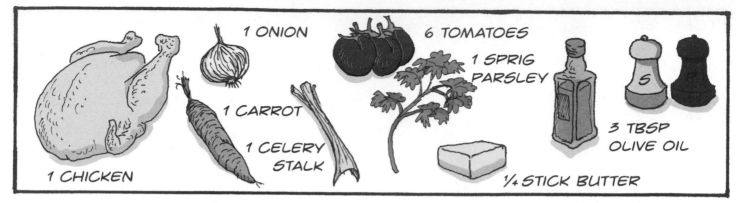

1 ONION
6 TOMATOES
1 SPRIG PARSLEY
1 CARROT
1 CELERY STALK
3 TBSP OLIVE OIL
1 CHICKEN
¼ STICK BUTTER

CHICKEN CACCIATORE

SERVES 4   PREP: 25 MIN   COOK: 1 HR

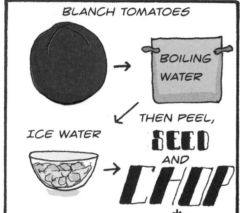

BLANCH TOMATOES

→ BOILING WATER

ICE WATER → THEN PEEL, **SEED** AND **CHOP**

CHOP CHOP CHOP

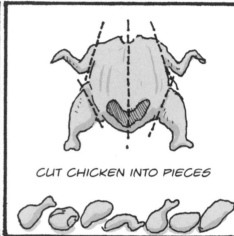

CUT CHICKEN INTO PIECES

HEAT

BUTTER + OIL

AND THEN ADD ONION

FLAMEPROOF DUTCH OVEN   MEDIUM HEAT

ADD CHICKEN AND STIR, TURNING FREQUENTLY, FOR 15 MIN UNTIL BROWNED

CARROT   CELERY

TOMATO

POUR IN ⅔ CUP WATER AND THEN COVER

AND SIMMER   FOR 45 MIN

60

ADD PARSLEY AND SEASON

1 CHICKEN

2¼ LB SEA SALT

1 EGG WHITE

1 SPRIG ROSEMARY

9 CUPS ALL-PURPOSE FLOUR

1 BAY LEAF

CHICKEN IN A SALT CRUST

SERVES 4   PREP: 30 MIN   COOK: 1½ HR

PREHEAT OVEN TO 325°F

MIX SALT AND FLOUR THEN...

...ADD THE EGG WHITE AND MIX THOROUGHLY

ADD HERBS

SEASON

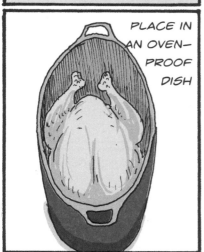

PLACE IN AN OVEN-PROOF DISH

COMPLETELY COVER WITH THE SALT MIXTURE

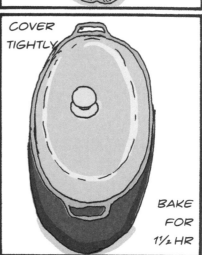

COVER TIGHTLY

BAKE FOR 1½ HR

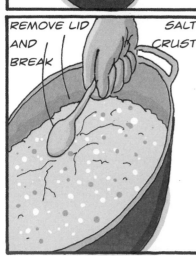

REMOVE LID AND BREAK   SALT CRUST

CUT INTO PIECES

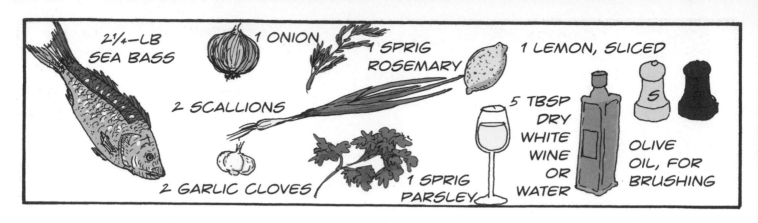

2¼-LB SEA BASS

1 ONION

1 SPRIG ROSEMARY

1 LEMON, SLICED

2 SCALLIONS

2 GARLIC CLOVES

1 SPRIG PARSLEY

5 TBSP DRY WHITE WINE OR WATER

OLIVE OIL, FOR BRUSHING

SEA BASS BAKED IN A PACKAGE

SERVES 4 PREP: 20 MIN COOK: 15 MIN

PREHEAT OVEN TO 400°F

TRIM SPINES, DESCALE, AND CLEAN THE SEA BASS, (SEE P. 95)

ONION — SLICE INTO RINGS

SCALLIONS — CHOP

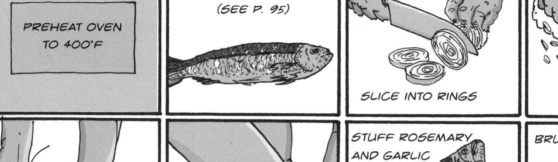

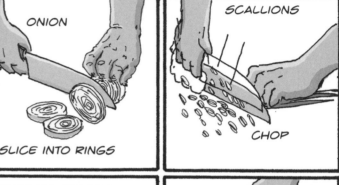

CHOP PARSLEY

SLICE 1 CLOVE GARLIC

STUFF ROSEMARY AND GARLIC CLOVE INTO CAVITY

BRUSH — WAX PAPER WITH OIL

BRUSH WITH OIL — SEASON

TOP WITH LEMON SLICES AND SPRINKLE WITH ONION, SCALLIONS, GARLIC, AND PARSLEY

SPOON OVER THE WINE

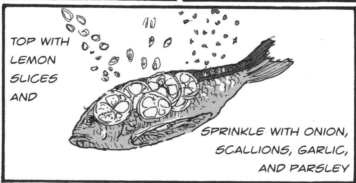

ENCLOSE IN THE PAPER

FOLD DOWN — TO SEAL

Bake FOR 15 MIN

1 CARROT

7 OZ GREEN BEANS

1 SPRIG ROSEMARY

2 TBSP OLIVE OIL

4 TUNA STEAKS

1 SHALLOT

7 OZ TURNIPS

1 SPRIG THYME

SCANT ½ CUP WHITE WINE OR WARM WATER

SLOW-COOKED TUNA

SERVES 4   PREP: 20 MIN   COOK: 55 MIN

CHOP

HALVE GREEN BEANS

HEAT OLIVE OIL THEN ADD TUNA AND COOK → UNTIL → BROWN ON BOTH SIDES

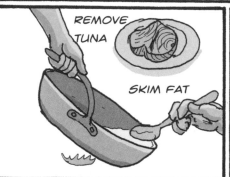

REMOVE TUNA

SKIM FAT

COOK SHALLOTS FOR ABOUT 5 MIN

THEN ADD CARROTS, TURNIPS, BEANS, THYME, AND ROSEMARY

MEDIUM HEAT

SEASON AND COOK FOR ABOUT 40 MIN

RETURN TUNA TO THE PAN

POUR IN WINE AND ⅔ CUP WARM WATER

COVER

AND SIMMER

FOR 30 MIN

DISCARD HERBS AND SERVE

63

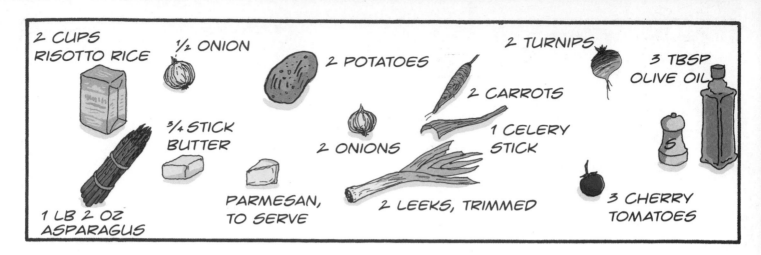

2 CUPS RISOTTO RICE

½ ONION

2 POTATOES

2 TURNIPS

2 CARROTS

3 TBSP OLIVE OIL

¾ STICK BUTTER

2 ONIONS

1 CELERY STICK

1 LB 2 OZ ASPARAGUS

PARMESAN, TO SERVE

2 LEEKS, TRIMMED

3 CHERRY TOMATOES

ASPARAGUS RISOTTO

SERVES 4   PREP: 1¼ HR   COOK: 30 MIN

STOCK

COARSELY CHOP

ADD PINCH SALT

POUR IN 6¼ CUPS WATER

BRING TO A BOIL THEN REDUCE HEAT AND SIMMER FOR 20 MIN

REMOVE FROM HEAT, STRAIN, AND KEEP LIQUID

CHOP REMAINING ONION

TRIM ENDS OF ASPARAGUS

BOIL ASPARAGUS FOR 5 MIN OR UNTIL TENDER

SALTED BOILING WATER

DRAIN AND CUT OFF ASPARAGUS TIPS

SET TIPS ASIDE

CHOP STEMS AND SET ASIDE

BRING STOCK TO A BOIL

AND MELT ¼ STICK BUTTER

HIGH HEAT   LOW HEAT

ADD ASPARAGUS TIPS AND COOK FOR 5 MIN STIRRING OCCASIONALLY THEN SET ASIDE

LOW HEAT

MELT OIL AND 1/4 STICK BUTTER

THEN ADD ONION

COOK FOR 5 MIN

LOW HEAT

STIR IN RICE   KEEP STIRRING UNTIL GRAINS ARE COATED IN FAT

ADD ASPARAGUS STEMS

ADD A LADLEFUL OF STOCK AND...

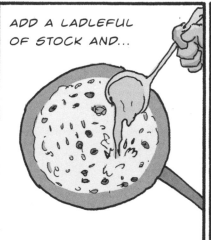

...COOK, STIRRING CONTINUOUSLY, UNTIL THE STOCK IS ABSORBED

KEEP ADDING STOCK...

...A LADLEFUL AT A TIME

AND KEEP STIRRING UNTIL ABSORBED...

THIS WILL TAKE 18-20 MIN

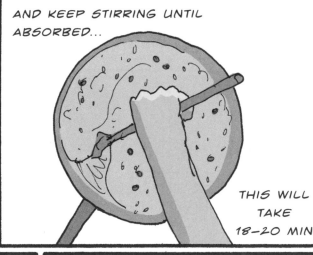

...AND THE RICE IS TENDER BUT STILL

al dente!

ITALIANS CALL THIS THE ALMA BIANCA (WHITE SOUL)

STIR IN REMAINING BUTTER AND THE ASPARAGUS TIPS

SERVE TOPPED WITH GRATED PARMESAN

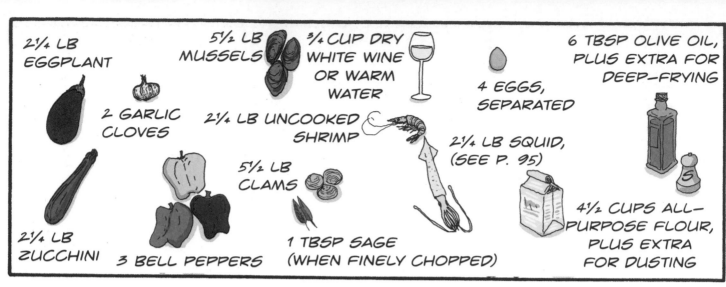

2¼ LB EGGPLANT

2 GARLIC CLOVES

2¼ LB ZUCCHINI

5½ LB MUSSELS

¾ CUP DRY WHITE WINE OR WARM WATER

2¼ LB UNCOOKED SHRIMP

5½ LB CLAMS

3 BELL PEPPERS

1 TBSP SAGE (WHEN FINELY CHOPPED)

4 EGGS, SEPARATED

2¼ LB SQUID, (SEE P. 95)

6 TBSP OLIVE OIL, PLUS EXTRA FOR DEEP-FRYING

4½ CUPS ALL-PURPOSE FLOUR, PLUS EXTRA FOR DUSTING

FRITTO MISTO

SERVES 16   PREP: 1½ HR   COOK: 30–40 MIN

SLICE EGGPLANT

CUT BELL PEPPERS INTO 1¼-INCH SQUARES

SLICE ZUCCHINI

SCRUB AND CLEAN CLAMS AND MUSSELS, DISCARDING ANY DAMAGED OR OPEN ONES (SEE P. 95)

CUT SQUID INTO RINGS

HEAT 3 TBSP OIL + 1 GARLIC CLOVE

ADD MUSSELS COVER, AND COOK FOR 4–5 MIN UNTIL SHELLS OPEN

REMOVE MUSSELS WITH A SLOTTED SPOON, DISCARD ANY THAT REMAIN SHUT, AND REMOVE REST FROM THEIR SHELLS

HEAT 3 TBSP OIL + 1 GARLIC CLOVE IN ANOTHER LARGE PAN

ADD CLAMS COVER COOK FOR 3–5 MIN UNTIL SHELLS OPEN

DISCARD ANY CLAMS THAT REMAIN SHUT REMOVE REST FROM THEIR SHELLS

COOK FOR 2 MIN SALTED BOILING WATER

DRAIN, PEEL, AND DE-VEIN SHRIMP (SEE P. 95)

(SEE P. 95)

BATTER

SIFT FLOUR

AND PINCH SALT

EGG YOLKS

ADD WINE OR WATER

STIR WELL

IN A DIFFERENT BOWL, WHISK THE EGG WHITES TO STIFF PEAKS

FOLD STIFF EGG WHITES AND THE SAGE INTO BATTER

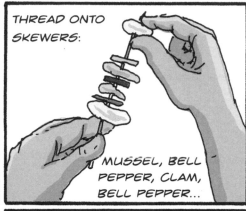

THREAD ONTO SKEWERS:

MUSSEL, BELL PEPPER, CLAM, BELL PEPPER...

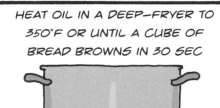

HEAT OIL IN A DEEP-FRYER TO 350°F OR UNTIL A CUBE OF BREAD BROWNS IN 30 SEC

DUST THE SQUID WITH FLOUR

THEN DEEP-FRY FOR 1-2 MIN

DIP SKEWERS IN BATTER AND DRAIN EXCESS

CAREFULLY

ADD SKEWERS TO HOT OIL AND DEEP-FRY UNTIL GOLDEN

DIP THE SHRIMP, EGGPLANT, AND ZUCCHINI INTO THE BATTER AND DEEP-FRY UNTIL GOLDEN

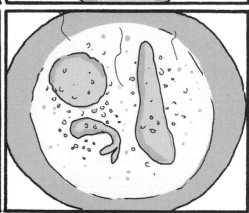

AS THE FRIED INGREDIENTS ARE READY, REMOVE WITH

A SLOTTED SPOON, DRAIN ON PAPER TOWELS, AND SEASON

PLACE ON A SERVING PLATE AND KEEP WARM UNTIL READY TO SERVE

1¾ CUPS ALL-PURPOSE FLOUR, PLUS EXTRA FOR DUSTING

1 TBSP CHOPPED MARJORAM

1½ CUPS ARUGULA

7 OZ TALEGGIO, DICED

¾ STICK BUTTER, CHILLED AND DICED, PLUS EXTRA FOR GREASING

1⅓ CUPS CREAM CHEESE

2 EGGS

1 TBSP POPPY SEEDS

2 TBSP BREADCRUMBS

ARUGULA & TALEGGIO PIE

SERVES 6   PREP: 15 MIN, PLUS 1 HR RESTING   COOK: 40 MIN

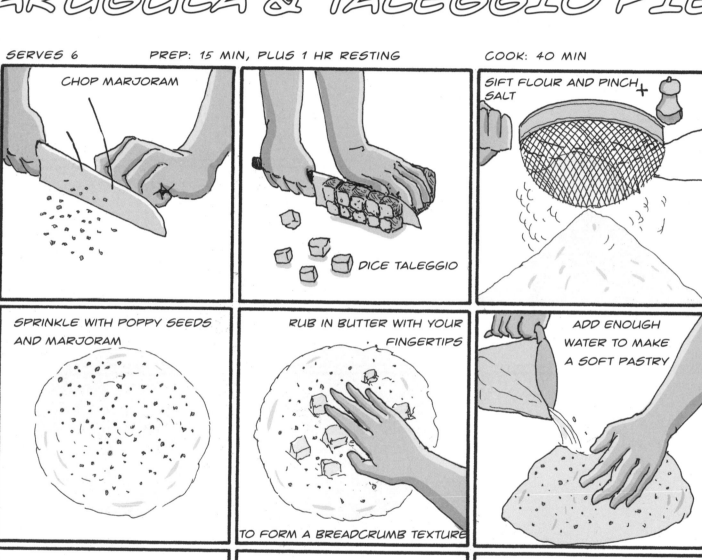

CHOP MARJORAM

DICE TALEGGIO

SIFT FLOUR AND PINCH SALT

SPRINKLE WITH POPPY SEEDS AND MARJORAM

RUB IN BUTTER WITH YOUR FINGERTIPS

TO FORM A BREADCRUMB TEXTURE

ADD ENOUGH WATER TO MAKE A SOFT PASTRY

THEN SHAPE INTO A BALL

COVER WITH PLASTIC WRAP AND LET REST FOR 1 HR

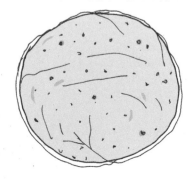

PREHEAT OVEN TO 350°F

GREASE AN 8-INCH TART PAN WITH BUTTER

68

BLANCH ARUGULA FOR 1 MIN

SALTED BOILING WATER

THEN DRAIN, LET COOL, AND SQUEEZE OUT LIQUID

BLITZ ARUGULA, BOTH CHEESES, BREAD—CRUMBS, AND EGGS IN A PROCESSOR AND SEASON

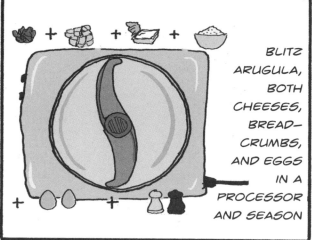

ROLL OUT PASTRY...

...AND USE IT TO LINE THE PREPARED PAN

TRIM EDGES OF PASTRY AND RESERVE TRIMMINGS

FILL WITH ARUGULA AND CHEESE MIXTURE

ROLL OUT THE TRIMMINGS

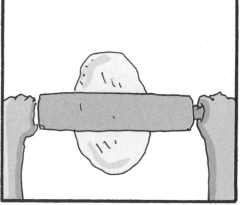

CUT INTO THIN STRIPS AND BRUSH THE ENDS WITH WATER

ARRANGE STRIPS IN A LATTICE OVER THE TOP OF THE PIE

Bake

FOR 40 MIN

CUT INTO WEDGES AND SERVE

69

DESSERTS & BAKING

1¾ CUPS ALL-PURPOSE FLOUR

2½ STICKS UNSALTED BUTTER

4½ OZ SEMISWEET CHOCOLATE, BROKEN INTO PIECES

SCANT ½ CUP SUPERFINE SUGAR

4 PEARS

SCANT ½ CUP HEAVY CREAM

4 TBSP GRAND MARNIER OR ORANGE JUICE

¼ CUP CHOPPED BLANCHED ALMONDS

CHOCOLATE & PEAR TART

SERVES 8   PREP: 1 HR, PLUS 1 HR STANDING & COOLING   COOK: 25 MIN

SIFT FLOUR, 1 TBSP SUGAR, AND PINCH SALT

ADD 1 STICK BUTTER

USING A CRISS-CROSS MOTION WITH 2 KNIVES, CUT THE BUTTER INTO THE FLOUR UNTIL PIECES ARE TINY

RUB IN THE BUTTER WITH FINGER-TIPS...

...UNTIL IT RESEMBLES FINE BREADCRUMBS

SPRINKLE 4–5 TBSP ICE WATER

STIR INTO MIXTURE TO FORM A DOUGH

SHAPE DOUGH INTO A FLAT DISC

COVER WITH PLASTIC WRAP

LEAVE TO STAND FOR 1 HR

MEANWHILE...

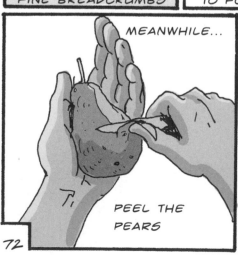

PEEL THE PEARS

HALVE AND CORE

SPRINKLE WITH SUGAR AND GRAND MARNIER

PREHEAT OVEN TO 350°F

ROLL OUT THE PASTRY UNTIL...

...¼ INCH THICK

LINE A 9-INCH TART PAN WITH THE PASTRY AND THEN LINE WITH FOIL

ALUMINUM FOIL

POUR IN PIE WEIGHTS

BAKE IN OVEN FOR 10 MIN

REMOVE FOIL AND WEIGHTS

PLACE PEARS IN PASTRY CASE

RETURN TO OVEN AND BAKE UNTIL PASTRY CRUST IS GOLDEN BROWN

REMOVE FROM OVEN THEN LET COOL

MELT CHOCOLATE WITH 1 TBSP WATER

LOW HEAT

ADD REMAINING BUTTER, MELT, THEN REMOVE FROM HEAT AND LET COOL

WHIP CREAM

FOLD CREAM INTO CHOCOLATE

COVER PEARS

SPRINKLE WITH ALMONDS AND SERVE

73

 4½ CUPS ALL-PURPOSE FLOUR

 1 TSP BAKING POWDER

 BUTTER, FOR GREASING

 2¼ CUPS SHELLED ALMONDS, IN THEIR SKINS

3 EGGS 2 EGG YOLKS

 PINCH OF SAFFRON THREADS, CRUSHED (OPTIONAL)

2½ CUPS SUPERFINE SUGAR

CANTUCCI

SERVES 4   PREP: 30 MIN   COOK: 30 MIN

PREHEAT OVEN TO 325°F

GREASE AND FLOUR

2 BAKING SHEETS

SIFT TOGETHER

FLOUR, SUGAR, BAKING POWDER, AND A PINCH SALT

 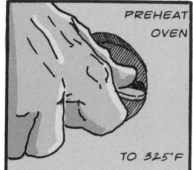 MAKE A WELL

ADD SAFFRON AND EGG YOLKS AND 2 EGGS

  INCORPORATE WITH FINGERS

ADD ALMONDS AND MIX

ROLL WITH FLOURED HANDS

1¼ INCH WIDE AND ½ INCH THICK

BEAT REMAINING EGG AND BRUSH ROLLS, THEN BAKE FOR 30 MINS

CUT AT AN ANGLE 1¼–1½ INCH THICK

THEN BAKE FOR ANOTHER 10–15 MIN

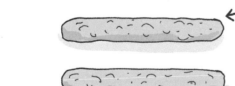 

LET COOL THEN STORE IN AN AIRTIGHT CONTAINER

6 EGGS

1¼ CUPS SUPERFINE SUGAR

1½ CUPS RASPBERRIES

3 CUPS HEAVY CREAM

RASPBERRY SEMIFREDDO

SERVES 6-8   PREP: 30 MIN, PLUS 4 HR FREEZING   COOK: 10-15 MIN

LINE AN 8-INCH LOAF PAN WITH PLASTIC WRAP

WHISK EGGS AND SUGAR IN HEATPROOF BOWL OVER PAN UNTIL THICK →

MUST NOT TOUCH WATER

BARELY SIMMERING WATER

← LOW HEAT

REMOVE FROM HEAT

CONTINUE WHISKING UNTIL THICKENED

MASH RASPBERRIES

WHIP CREAM TO STIFF PEAKS

STIR EGG MIXTURE

AND RASPBERRIES INTO CREAM

POUR MIXTURE INTO TIN

FREEZE FOR AT LEAST 4 HR

SERVE IN SLICES

¾ STICK UNSALTED BUTTER, SOFTENED, PLUS EXTRA FOR GREASING

WHIPPED CREAM, TO SERVE (OPTIONAL)

1¾ CUPS SELF-RISING FLOUR

¾ CUP SUPERFINE SUGAR

3 APPLES

3 EGGS, AT ROOM TEMPERATURE

APPLE CAKE

SERVES 6   PREP: 35 MIN, PLUS COOLING   COOK: 40 MIN

PREHEAT OVEN TO 350°F

GREASE AN 8-INCH CAKE PAN

PEEL AND CORE...

...THEN CHOP

3 EGGS + SUGAR

WHISK UNTIL PALE AND FLUFFY AND THICK ENOUGH TO LEAVE A RIBBON

...ABOUT 10-12 MIN

THEN BEAT IN 1 TBSP BUTTER

DON'T WORRY IF MIXTURE LOOKS LUMPY!

ADD FLOUR IN 2 PARTS, ALTERNATING WITH THE APPLES

MIX GENTLY THEN TRANSFER TO THE PAN

Bake

FOR 40 MIN THEN LET COOL

TURN OUT...

...AND SERVE WITH WHIPPED CREAM IF YOU LIKE

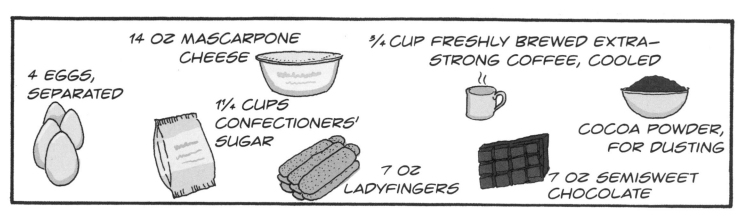

TIRAMISU

SERVES 6 | PREP: 15 MINS, PLUS 3 HR CHILLING

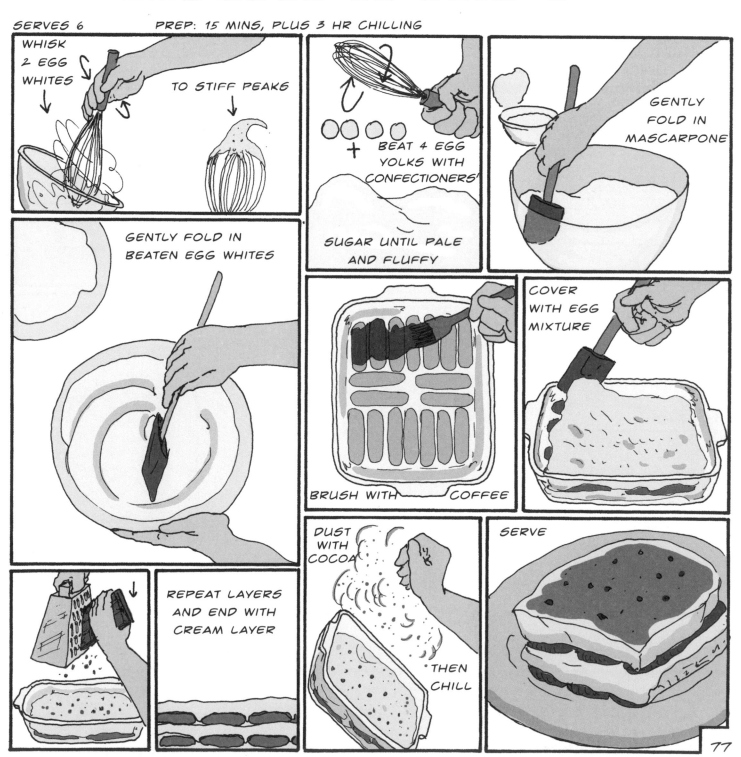

WHISK 2 EGG WHITES

TO STIFF PEAKS

BEAT 4 EGG YOLKS WITH CONFECTIONERS' SUGAR UNTIL PALE AND FLUFFY

GENTLY FOLD IN MASCARPONE

GENTLY FOLD IN BEATEN EGG WHITES

BRUSH WITH COFFEE

COVER WITH EGG MIXTURE

REPEAT LAYERS AND END WITH CREAM LAYER

DUST WITH COCOA

THEN CHILL

SERVE

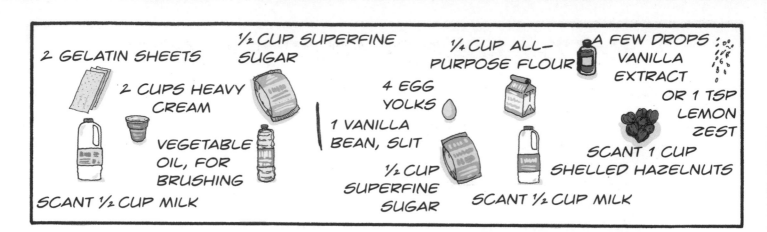

PANNA COTTA

SERVES 6   PREP: 35 MIN, PLUS COOLING   COOK: 40 MIN

SOAK GELATIN LEAVES IN WATER FOR 3-5 MIN

HEAT SCANT ½ CUP MILK TO JUST BELOW SIMMERING POINT

↓

TAKE CARE NOT TO LET IT BOIL

← LOW HEAT

THEN REMOVE MILK FROM HEAT, DRAIN GELATIN SHEETS AND ADD TO MILK

POUR CREAM INTO A SEPARATE PAN

ADD VANILLA BEAN AND ½ CUP SUGAR TO CREAM

AND BOIL OVER LOW HEAT, STIRRING CONTINUOUSLY

REMOVE FROM HEAT AND REMOVE VANILLA BEAN

STIR MILK AND GELATIN MIXTURE INTO VANILLA CREAM MIXTURE

BRUSH MOLDS WITH OIL

POUR IN MIXTURE

AND CHILL FOR AT LEAST 4 HR

WITH HAZELNUT SAUCE

PREHEAT OVEN TO 400°F

BEAT EGG YOLKS WITH ½ CUP SUPERFINE SUGAR UNTIL PALE AND FLUFFY

GRADUALLY STIR IN FLOUR AND TRANSFER TO A PAN

IN ANOTHER PAN BRING MILK JUST TO BOILING POINT THEN ADD VANILLA OR LEMON ZEST AND...

...REMOVE FROM HEAT

...GRADUALLY ADD THE HOT MILK TO EGG MIXTURE STIRRING CONSTANTLY FOR 3-4 MIN...

LOW HEAT

...UNTIL THICK, THEN POUR CUSTARD INTO A BOWL AND LET COOL

SPREAD OUT HAZELNUTS ON BAKING SHEET AND ROAST FOR ABOUT 10 MIN WITHOUT BROWNING

TIP ONTO CLEAN DISH TOWEL AND RUB TO REMOVE SKIN

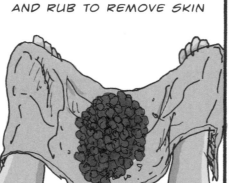

FINELY CRUSH THE HAZELNUTS IN A MORTAR WITH A PESTLE

THEN STIR INTO THE COOLED CUSTARD

UNMOLD THE PANNA COTTA ONTO A PLATE, POUR OVER SOME HAZELNUT SAUCE, AND SERVE

2 CUPS MASCARPONE CHEESE

3/4 CUP SUPERFINE SUGAR

1 CUP CREAM CHEESE

1/2 TSP GRATED LEMON ZEST

1 TSP VANILLA EXTRACT

 1/4 CUP CORNSTARCH

4 EGGS

SCANT 1 CUP SOUR CREAM

 STRAWBERRIES, TO SERVE

MASCARPONE DESSERT

SERVES 6   PREP: 35 MIN, PLUS COOLING   COOK: 40 MIN

PREHEAT OVEN TO 350°F

LINE A 10-INCH PAN WITH PARCHMENT PAPER

 VANILLA

LEMON ZEST + SUGAR + BOTH CHEESES AND BEAT

 *When Smooth*

GRADUALLY ADD EGGS

 SIFT IN CORNSTARCH

THEN BEAT AGAIN

REDUCE HEAT TO 275°F

AND BAKE FOR 1 HR THEN TURN OVEN OFF

LET STAND FOR 1 HR

 COOL ON A RACK

Chill

IN FRIDGE FOR 2 HR THEN TURN OUT

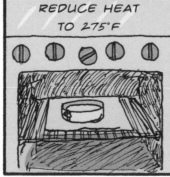 SPREAD OVER THIN LAYER OF SOUR CREAM

 SERVE WITH STRAWBERRIES

¼ CUP SUPERFINE SUGAR, PLUS EXTRA FOR SPRINKLING

1¼ CUPS MILK

1 VANILLA BEAN, SLIT

SCANT ⅓ CUP ALL-PURPOSE FLOUR

1½ OZ TORRONE (ITALIAN NOUGAT)

¼ STICK UNSALTED BUTTER, PLUS EXTRA FOR GREASING

4 EGG YOLKS AND 5 EGG WHITES

TORRONE SOUFFLÉ

SERVES 6   PREP: 50 MIN, PLUS 30 MIN INFUSING   COOK: 40 MIN

FINELY CHOP NOUGAT

PREHEAT OVEN TO 400°F AND PREPARE 6 RAMEKINS

GREASE THEN SPRINKLE WITH SUGAR

BRING 1 CUP MILK TO THE BOIL THEN REMOVE FROM HEAT

SUGAR + PINCH SALT + VANILLA BEAN

COVER AND INFUSE FOR 15 MIN

THEN REMOVE BEAN

MIX FLOUR AND REMAINING MILK IN A NEW PAN

BRING TO THE BOIL

STIR RAPIDLY

POUR IN THE VANILLA MILK AND STIR AGAIN

WHEN THICK, REMOVE FROM HEAT

LET COOL THEN ADD 4 YOLKS, 1 AT A TIME

ADD BUTTER AND TORRONE... AND STIR IN

WHISK THE 5 EGG WHITES...

...TO STIFF PEAKS

FOLD WHITES INTO MILK MIXTURE

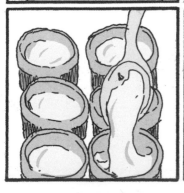

Bake

FOR 30 MIN

SERVE HOT

9 OZ STRAWBERRIES

¾ CUP SUPERFINE SUGAR

1 ORANGE

1 LEMON

STRAWBERRY GRANITA

SERVES 4   PREP: 35 MIN, PLUS COOLING   COOK: 40 MIN

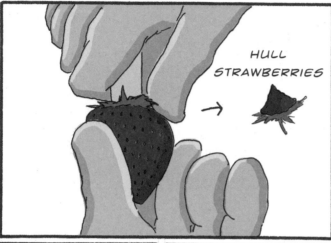

HULL STRAWBERRIES

JUICE LEMON AND ORANGE

HEAT SUGAR AND 1 CUP WATER

BRING TO A BOIL STIR UNTIL SUGAR DISSOLVES

BOIL OVER LOW HEAT FOR ABOUT 5–10 MIN

UNTIL SYRUPY

REMOVE FROM THE HEAT AND LET COOL

SET ASIDE 4 STRAWBERRIES

PUSH THE REMAINDER THROUGH A NYLON STRAINER INTO A BOWL

POUR IN LEMON AND ORANGE JUICE AND STIR

ADD THE SYRUP AND STIR

POUR MIXTURE INTO A FREEZERPROOF CONTAINER...

...THEN FREEZE FOR ABOUT 3 HR...

Stir

EVERY 30 MIN

SPOON INTO 4 TALL GLASSES...

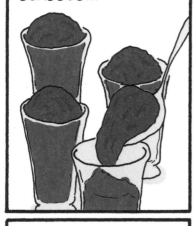

...AND DECORATE WITH A STRAWBERRY

FOR AN APRICOT VERSION:

1 CUP SUPERFINE SUGAR
14 OZ APRICOTS, PITTED AND CHOPPED
1 TSP VANILLA EXTRACT
JUICE OF 1 LEMON, STRAINED
8 MINT LEAVES

BRING SUGAR AND 1 CUP WATER TO A BOIL AND STIR UNTIL SUGAR DISSOLVES THEN ADD APRICOTS AND SIMMER GENTLY FOR 30 MIN

LOW HEAT

REMOVE FROM HEAT AND LET COOL

THEN PUSH APRICOTS AND SYRUP THROUGH A NYLON STRAINER INTO A BOWL

STIR IN VANILLA EXTRACT AND LEMON JUICE

POUR MIXTURE INTO A FREEZERPROOF CONTAINER

FREEZE FOR 3 HR STIRRING EVERY 30 MIN

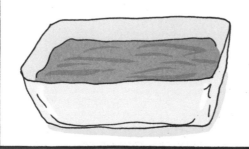

SPOON INTO 4 TALL GLASSES

AND DECORATE WITH 2 MINT LEAVES

83

½ STICK UNSALTED BUTTER, MELTED, PLUS EXTRA FOR GREASING

VANILLA BEAN

5 EGGS, SEPARATED

3 TBSP CORNSTARCH

3½ OZ SEMISWEET CHOCOLATE, BROKEN INTO PIECES

¼ CUP ALL-PURPOSE FLOUR, PLUS EXTRA FOR DUSTING

2 TBSP SUPERFINE SUGAR

1¾ CUPS CONFECTIONERS' SUGAR

CHOCOLATE DELIGHT

SERVES 4–6   PREP: 50 MIN, PLUS COOLING   COOK: 40 MIN

FOR THE VANILLA SUGAR

VANILLA BEAN

COVER WITH SUPERFINE SUGAR

SEAL WITH A LID

STORE IN A COOL PLACE FOR 2–3 DAYS BEFORE USING

PREHEAT OVEN TO 300°F AND PREPARE A CAKE PAN

MELT BUTTER

LOW HEAT

MELT CHOCOLATE IN HEATPROOF BOWL

MUST NOT TOUCH WATER

BARELY SIMMERING WATER

DUST...  ...WITH FLOUR

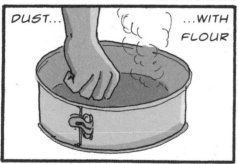

VANILLA SUGAR + HALF THE CONFECTIONERS' SUGAR

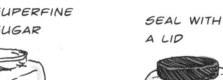

EGG YOLKS

AND BEAT

BEAT IN BUTTER AND CHOCOLATE

SIFT IN FLOUR AND CORNSTARCH AND MIX WELL

WHISK EGG WHITES TO STIFF PEAKS

WHISK IN REMAINING CONFECTIONERS' SUGAR

GENTLY FOLD IN CHOCOLATE MIXTURE

POUR INTO PREPARED TIN

Bake

FOR 40 MIN

REMOVE FROM OVEN AND COOL ON A WIRE RACK

Chill

IN THE FRIDGE BEFORE TURNING OUT

CUT INTO WEDGES AND SERVE

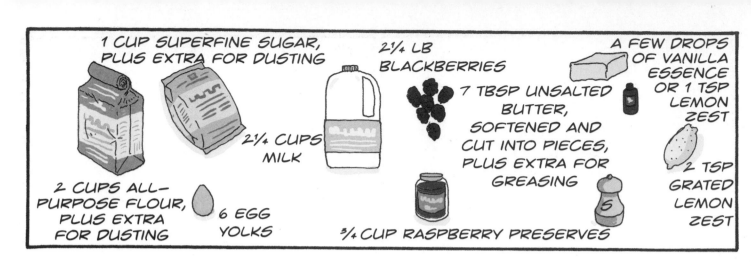

1 CUP SUPERFINE SUGAR, PLUS EXTRA FOR DUSTING

2 CUPS ALL-PURPOSE FLOUR, PLUS EXTRA FOR DUSTING

2¼ CUPS MILK

6 EGG YOLKS

2¼ LB BLACKBERRIES

7 TBSP UNSALTED BUTTER, SOFTENED AND CUT INTO PIECES, PLUS EXTRA FOR GREASING

¾ CUP RASPBERRY PRESERVES

A FEW DROPS OF VANILLA ESSENCE OR 1 TSP LEMON ZEST

2 TSP GRATED LEMON ZEST

BLACKBERRY TART

SERVES 6   PREP: 2½ HR   COOK: 45–60 MIN

TO MAKE THE PIE CRUST DOUGH...

SIFT 1¾ CUP FLOUR ½ CUP SUGAR INTO A MOUND

EGG YOLKS +  + BUTTER

2 TSP LEMON ZEST AND PINCH SALT

MIX THOROUGHLY

KNEAD

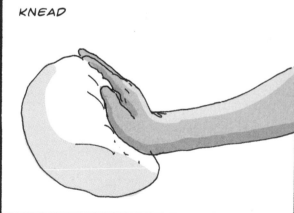

WRAP IN PLASTIC WRAP

AND CHILL IN FRIDGE FOR 1 HR

MEANWHILE MAKE THE...

CUSTARD

BEAT EGG YOLKS + SUGAR IN A PAN

UNTIL PALE AND FLUFFY

GRADUALLY STIR IN FLOUR

IN ANOTHER PAN BRING MILK TO A BOIL

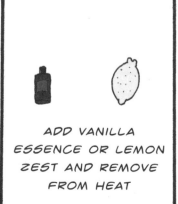

ADD VANILLA ESSENCE OR LEMON ZEST AND REMOVE FROM HEAT

SLOWLY POUR HOT MILK INTO THE EGG MIXTURE AND COOK UNTIL THICKENED, 3–4 MIN

LOW HEAT

POUR INTO A HEATPROOF BOWL AND LET COOL, STIRRING FROM TIME TO TIME

PREHEAT OVEN TO 350°F

GREASE AN 11–INCH TART PAN

WITH BUTTER

ROLL OUT PASTRY...

...ON A LIGHTLY FLOURED SURFACE

LINE PAN WITH PASTRY AND PRICK BASE WITH A FORK

POUR IN COOLED CUSTARD

Bake

FOR 35–40 MIN

MEANWHILE, RESERVE 3 CUPS BLACKBERRIES

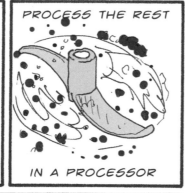

PROCESS THE REST IN A PROCESSOR

BLACKBERRY PUREE JAM

MIX IN A BOWL

REMOVE TART FROM OVEN AND LET COOL ON WIRE RACK

SPREAD BLACKBERRY MIXTURE OVER THE BAKED CUSTARD

...AND SERVE

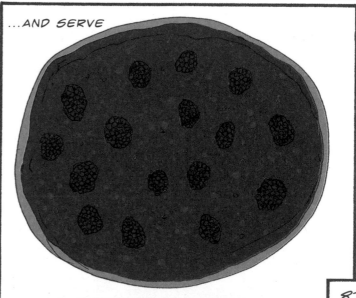

TOP WITH RESERVED BLACKBERRIES

1 LB 2 OZ FRUITS OF THE FOREST

(SUCH AS STRAWBERRIES, BLACKBERRIES, RASPBERRIES, AND BLUEBERRIES)

3 EGG YOLKS

⅓ CUP SUPERFINE SUGAR

2 TBSP GRAND MARNIER (OPTIONAL)

½ LEMON

FOREST FRUITS WITH ZABAGLIONE

SERVES 4   PREP: 20 MIN   COOK: 30 MIN

ZEST LEMON

HULL STRAWBERRIES AND CUT ANY LARGE BERRIES IN HALF

DIVIDE BERRIES AMONG 4 HEATPROOF DISHES

PREHEAT THE BROILER

EGG YOLKS

+ SUGAR

+ GRAND MARNIER

WHISK TOGETHER IN A HEATPROOF BOWL

COOK FOR ABOUT 8–10 MIN, UNTIL THICKENED

WHISKING CONSTANTLY

MUST NOT TOUCH WATER

BARELY SIMMERING WATER

THEN REMOVE FROM HEAT AND ADD LEMON ZEST

SPOON ZABAGLIONE OVER THE BERRIES

PLACE DISHES UNDER BROILER AND BROIL UNTIL GOLDEN ON TOP

SERVE HOT OR COLD

 5 YELLOW PEACHES

¼ STICK UNSALTED BUTTER, PLUS EXTRA FOR GREASING

 ¼ CUP SUPERFINE SUGAR

 2 EGG YOLKS

 ¼ CUP UNSWEETENED COCOA POWDER

4 AMARETTI COOKIES, CRUSHED

STUFFED PEACHES

SERVES 4   PREP: 20 MIN   COOK: 30 MIN

PRE HEAT
OVEN TO 325°F

GREASE OVENPROOF DISH
WITH BUTTER

PEEL   HALVE
1 PEACH
PIT
CHOP

PUT THE CHOPPED FLESH IN A BOWL

HALVE AND PIT REMAINING PEACHES

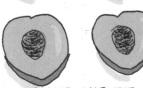

SCOOP OUT A LITTLE FLESH FROM THE CAVITY OF EACH PEACH AND ADD TO THE BOWL
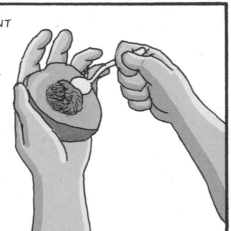

ADD SUGAR, COCOA POWDER + CRUSHED + AMARETTI + EGG YOLKS

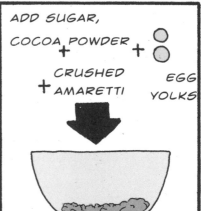

SPOON THE MIXTURE INTO THE PEACH CAVITIES
AND PILE UP INTO A DOME

DOT EACH WITH BUTTER
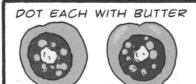

Bake
FOR 1 HOUR

SERVE WARM

Ingredients

- 2–3 TBSP WHITE RUM
- 1¼ CUPS ALL-PURPOSE FLOUR, PLUS EXTRA FOR DUSTING
- 1 TBSP LARD
- 1 EGG WHITE, PLUS EXTRA FOR BRUSHING
- 1 TSP SUPERFINE SUGAR
- 2 TSP WHITE WINE VINEGAR
- 2¼ LB RICOTTA ROMANA
- 3¼ CUPS CONFECTIONERS' SUGAR, PLUS EXTRA FOR DUSTING
- VEGETABLE OIL, FOR FRYING
- 4–5 PISTACHIOS, SLIVERED
- 3 OZ CHOCOLATE, CHOPPED
- ¾ TBSP MALVASIA WINE (OPTIONAL)
- ⅓ CUP CANDIED PUMPKIN, DICED

CANNOLI

MAKES 20–22   PREP: 30 MIN, PLUS STANDING & CHILLING TIME   COOK: 1 HR

Filling

PIPING BAG

PRESS RICOTTA THROUGH A STRAINER INTO A BOWL

ADD CONFECTIONERS' SUGAR AND BEAT

WITH A WOODEN SPOON

PUMPKIN + CHOCOLATE + RUM

MIX WELL

COVER WITH PLASTIC WRAP AND CHILL IN FRIDGE FOR 12 HR

DOUGH

SIFT FLOUR + PINCH SALT

ADD LARD, VINEGAR, WINE, EGG WHITE, SUPERFINE SUGAR, AND MIX WELL UNTIL FIRM

SHAPE INTO A BALL

COVER WITH PLASTIC WRAP AND STAND FOR 30 MIN

CUT DOUGH INTO 3 PIECES

ROLL OUT ON A LIGHTLY...

...FLOURED COUNTER

CUT OUT 20-22 SQUARES

PLACE A CANNOLI TUBE (SEE, P. 96)

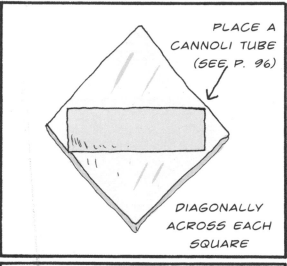

DIAGONALLY ACROSS EACH SQUARE

WRAP DOUGH AROUND TUBE

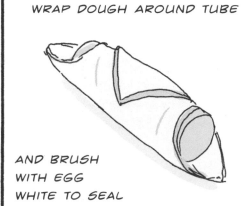

AND BRUSH WITH EGG WHITE TO SEAL

THREE-QUARTERS FILL A SKILLET WITH OIL AND HEAT

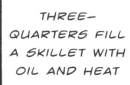

WHEN A CUBE OF BREAD BROWNS IN 30 SEC...

...CAREFULLY ADD THE CANNOLI A FEW AT A TIME

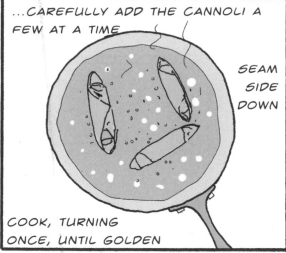

SEAM SIDE DOWN

COOK, TURNING ONCE, UNTIL GOLDEN

REMOVE WITH A SLOTTED SPOON

DRAIN ON PAPER TOWELS

LET COOL THEN CAREFULLY REMOVE THE METAL TUBES AND LET COOL COMPLETELY

WATCH OUT, THE TUBES MAY BE HOT!

FILL PIPING BAG WITH RICOTTA MIXTURE AND THEN PIPE INTO THE CANNOLI

DUST WITH CONFECTIONERS' SUGAR

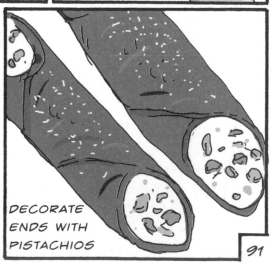

DECORATE ENDS WITH PISTACHIOS

RECIPE NOTES

Butter should always be unsalted.

Herbs are always fresh, unless otherwise specified.

Pepper is always freshly ground black pepper, unless otherwise specified.

Eggs, vegetables, and fruits are assumed to be medium size, unless otherwise specified.

Milk is always whole, unless otherwise specified.

Garlic cloves are assumed to be large; use two if yours are small.

Ham means cooked ham, unless otherwise specified.

A number of the recipes include alcohol, which can easily be replaced with water, stock, or, if a dessert, orange juice.

Prosciutto refers exclusively to raw, dry-cured ham, usually from Parma or San Daniele in northern Italy.

Cooking and preparation times are for guidance only, as individual ovens vary. If using a convection oven, follow the manufacturer's instructions concerning oven temperatures.

To test whether your deep-frying oil is hot enough, add a cube of stale bread. If it browns in thirty seconds, the temperature is 350–375°F, about right for most frying. Exercise caution when deep frying: Add the food carefully to avoid splashing, wear long sleeves, and never leave the pan unattended.

Some recipes include raw or very lightly cooked eggs, such as Tiramisu (p. 77). These should be avoided particularly by the elderly, infants, pregnant women, convalescents, and anyone with an impaired immune system.

TECHNIQUES IN DETAIL

FISH (DE-SCALE & CLEAN)

Scrape off the scales of a fish by working from tail to head, using the back of a knife. Trim away the fins. Insert the point of your knife in the belly button (about two-thirds along) and cut along the belly. Scoop out the entrails with your hand. Rinse.

KNEAD

Pushing, pulling, and folding dough over itself for several minutes to work in air and make it elastic. Best done on a lightly floured counter. Alternatively, an electric stand mixer fitted with a dough hook may be used. Pasta and yeast doughs are kneaded vigorously, whereas pastry dough is kneaded lightly and only briefly.

MUSSELS (CLEAN & PREP)

Scrub the mussels hard under running water with a scourer or knife to remove any barnacles. Pull away the hairy bit known as the "beard." Rinse well. The shells should be closed. If there are open shells, tap them—they will close if they are still alive. If a shell does not close, discard it.

SHRIMP (PREP)

It's not essential to de-vein prawns (removing the dark vein that runs along the back) but the vein can be gritty and unpleasant to eat. Remove the head from the body and peel the body shell away. Cut along the back with a sharp knife just far enough in to reveal the vein, then pull this out and discard it.

SARDINES (SCALE, CLEAN, & BONE)

Scrape off the scales from tail to head with the back of a knife (see De-Scale & Clean Fish). Supporting the back of the fish with your free hand, insert the tip of the knife at the tail end and run it up the length of the body. Remove and discard the guts and rinse well. Pull away the gills and rinse the fish to remove the blood line. Turn the fish on its back, and with your finger, gently loosen the bones close to the backbone and release the fine bones away from the flesh. Lift up the bone, and using scissors, snip the bone at the tail end and discard. Remove any remaining pin bones with tweezers.

SQUID (PREP)

Squid is often sold cleaned and prepared. If not, it is simple to clean and prepare at home. Hold the squid head in one hand and the tentacles in another. Pull firmly to separate. Cut the tentacles away from the intestine just below the eye of the squid and remove the soft skeleton (beak) at the center of the tentacles. Rinse.

WHISK/BEAT

Mixing with a balloon or electric whisk, handheld mixer, or an electric stand mixer to make ingredients such as eggs, butter, or cream light and frothy. If whisking egg whites, especially for a soufflé, do be sure to use a clean, dry bowl.

GLOSSARY

AL DENTE
Essential Italian term for cooking pasta until tender but still firm to the bite.

BAKE IN A PACKAGE
Wrapping fish, meat, or vegetables in a pocket of aluminum foil or parchment paper before cooking to keep it juicy.

BÉCHAMEL
A white sauce made using a roux (a paste) of equal parts butter and flour, then whisking in milk over the heat until you get a thick, creamy sauce.

BLANCH
Briefly plunging fruit or vegetables into boiling water to soften but not completely cook them.

BLEND
Whizzing together ingredients in an electric blender or food processor until creamy or chopped to a pulp.

BOIL
Cooking ingredients for a specified length of time in water or stock that is bubbling vigorously.

BOLOGNESE
Meaning "from the city of Bologna," it can refer to any dish from that region, such as ragú (meat sauce), tagliatelle, or lasagna.

BREAD/BREADCRUMBS
Dipping fish, meat or vegetables in whisked egg, then in breadcrumbs, before frying until crisp and golden.

BROWN IN AN OVEN
Popping something like lasagna into a hot oven for five to ten minutes until it's golden brown and bubbling on top.

BROWN IN A PAN
Cooking meat or vegetables (like garlic or onions) in butter or oil over medium heat until they are golden and shimmering.

BRUSCHETTA
A slice of lightly toasted, stale bread rubbed with garlic, drizzled with oil, and most commonly topped with chopped tomatoes.

CACCIATORE
A 'hunter's style' one-pot casserole of chicken or rabbit cooked with onions and mushrooms, or tomatoes, bell peppers, and carrots.

CANNOLI TUBE
Tubes around which cannoli dough is wrapped before deep frying. Usually made of metal, they are available at good kitchenware stores.

CAPONATA
Sicilian *antipasto* of diced eggplant, bell peppers, and tomatoes slowly stewed in a sweet-and-sour sauce of vinegar, raisins, and capers.

CARVE

Slicing roast meat with a long, sharp knife, using a long-handled, two-pronged fork to hold it steady. Easiest if the meat has been left to stand for ten to fifteen minutes after it comes out of the oven.

CHOP

Chopping ingredients into bite-size chunks.

COCOTTE

Cooking something slowly in a thick porcelain ramekin or terra-cotta pot.

COOK OVER LOW HEAT

Getting something meltingly tender by turning the heat to its lowest setting and cooking for a long time.

COOK UNTIL SOFTENED

Usually applies to vegetables such as onions that need to be cooked down until soft, sweet, and translucent.

COVER

Placing a lid over the top of a pan or dish to seal in moisture and stop ingredients from drying out.

COVER WITH A THIN LAYER

Just covering the contents of a dish with a thin layer of cream, gelatin, or sauce.

CRUSH

Smashing garlic with the back of a knife, or grinding spices in a pestle and mortar.

CUT INTO PORTIONS

Dividing meat, poultry, or fish into one-person-size pieces.

DEEP FRY

Bringing a pan of fat or oil (vegetable is best) to a boil for deep frying. Add a cube of stale bread. If it browns in thirty seconds, the oil is ready.

DUST WITH FLOUR

Lightly coating ingredients with flour before frying to make them crunchier.

EVAPORATE

Allowing excess liquid to bubble off a sauce in order to thicken it.

FILL

Stuffing pastry shells with, for example, eggs or fruit, or layering cakes with cream or jelly.

FOLD

Gently mixing flour with cutting movements into liquids (eggs and sugar) with a stainless-steel spoon or knife.

GARNISH

The final decoration before a dish is served. Herbs, lemon slices, and salad are common examples.

GREASE

Rubbing oil, butter, or fat into a baking pan or mold to stop a mixture sticking when you cook it.

MALVASIA WINE

A group of wine grape varieties grown in the Mediterranean. The sweet variety is used in desserts, such as Cannoli (pp. 90–91). Madeira may be used as an altenative.

MASCARPONE

A creamy, fresh Italian cheese from the Lombardy region, similar to cream cheese, but with a tangy and nutty flavor. Most often used for desserts, such as Tiramisu (p. 77).

MILANESE

Fillets or chops of chicken or veal (occasionally vegetables) breaded and sautéed in butter until crisp.

MORTAR & PESTLE

Utensil used for grinding spices or pounding pesto to a puree. A blender can be used instead.

MOUND

Sifting flour directly onto a counter into a pyramid shape for making pasta.

PANCETTA

Cured, salted, or smoked pork belly, great for flavoring the base of sauces.

PASSATA

Canned, crushed, and sieved tomatoes (less concentrated than tomato puree).

PIE WEIGHTS

Pea-size, ceramic weights used to line uncooked pastry cases for pre-cooking.

POLENTA

Ground corn that can be served like a mash or set into wedges and baked or broiled.

PORCINI

Large, brown-cap mushrooms with lots of flesh and little gill.

POUND

Softening meat or vegetable fibers by battering them with something heavy, such as a meat mallet or a rolling pin.

PRE—HEAT

Bringing the oven to a specified temperature before you start cooking.

PROSCIUTTO

Cured ham, the best of which comes from Parma.

RIBOLLITA

Meaning "reboiled." A warming Tuscan stew based on *cavolo nero* (Tuscan cabbage) and white beans, usually reheated and eaten the day after making.

RICOTTA ROMANA

An Italian curd cheese made from the whey from whole sheep's milk. It has a rich but delicate flavor that is sweeter than that of other types of ricotta.

SALSA VERDE

Tangy green sauce of capers and herbs for serving with grilled fish or meat.

SEED

Scraping out and discarding the seeds from, for example, a red bell pepper or a chile.

SEMIFREDDO

Quick-to-make, semi-frozen soft ice cream.

SHRED

Finely cutting ingredients like cabbage and lettuce into thin strips.

SIMMER

Bringing liquid down to just below boiling point or to turn down the heat under a liquid that has reached boiling point so that the surface of the liquid barely ripples.

SOAK

Softening dried fruits, vegetables, or fungi such as mushrooms in water to plump up before cooking.

SPRINKLE

Adding one ingredient slowly to another, or scattering an ingredient over a work counter.

STICKS

Vegetables cut into long, thin, rectangular pieces about the diameter of a pencil.

STIR IN BUTTER OR CREAM

Adding butter or cream at the end of a dish to give a rich, velvety, and shiny finish.

STUFF

Putting savory ingredients like rice or breadcrumbs into another ingredient, such as hollowed-out tomatoes or chicken.

TALEGGIO

Named after Val Taleggio in northern Italy, this soft, creamy cheese has a strong aroma but a mild, fruity flavor.

TIE MEAT

Wrapping meat in butchers' string to hold in shape while cooking.

YEAST, FRESH/DRY

For rising bread dough or other baked goods. Note that while dried yeast can be added directly to flour, fresh yeast needs first to be mixed with water.

MENU IDEAS

SPRING MENU

Broiled Stuffed Squid, p. 17

·

Potato & Spinach Gnocchi,
p. 39

·

Chicken Stuffed with
Mascarpone, pp. 54–55

·

Panna Cotta with
Hazelnut Sauce, pp. 78–79

SUMMER MENU

Tomato Bruschetta, p. 22

·

Linguine with Pesto, p. 46

·

Sea Bass Baked
in a Package, p. 62

·

Cannoli, pp. 90–91

FALL MENU

Stuffed Porcini
Mushrooms, pp. 14–15

·

Tagliatelle with
Peas & Ham, p. 38

·

Slow-Cooked Tuna, p. 63

·

Apple Cake, p. 76

WINTER MENU

Ribollita, p. 28

·

Cheese- & Vegetable-
Filled Ravioli, pp. 44–45

·

Chicken Cacciatore,
p. 60

·

Tiramisu, p. 77

QUICK WEEKNIGHT SUPPER

Eggs en Cocotte, p. 19

·

Fusilli with
Mushrooms, p. 40

·

Forest Fruits
with Zabaglione, p. 88

LIGHT LUNCH

Spinach Salad
with Bacon & Beans,
p. 31

·

Mussels Marinara,
p. 53

·

Strawberry or Apricot
Granita, pp. 82–83

BIRTHDAY DINNER

Pizza Margherita,
pp. 21–22

·

Farfalle with
Shrimp, p. 47

·

Grilled Sardines, p. 58

·

Stuffed Peaches,
p. 89

DINING ALFRESCO

Panzanella, p. 30

·

Rigatoni with
Meatballs, p. 42

·

Fritto Misto, pp. 66–67

·

Raspberry
Semifreddo, p. 75

INDEX

Phaidon Press Limited
65 Bleecker Street
New York, NY 10012

www.phaidon.com

First published 2014
© 2014 Phaidon Press Limited
ISBN: 978 0 7148 6820 2 *56031601*
(US Edition)

3/15

Chop, Sizzle, Wow originates from *Il cucchiaio d'argento*,
first published in 1950, eighth edition (revised, expanded
and updated in 1997), and *Il cucchiaio d'argento estate*, first
published in 2005. © Editoriale Domus S.p.a

A CIP catalogue record for this book is available from
the British Library.

Commissioning Editors: Emma Robertson
& Emilia Terragni
Project Editor: Sophie Hodgkin
Production Controller: Adela Cory

Introduction by Tara Stevens
Inked Illustrations by Adriano de Campos Rampazzo
Illustration colour by Colin White
Design by Julia Hasting
Layout by Hans Stofregen & Colin White

Printed in Romania